A Pilgrim's Guide to
THE LANDS OF ST PAUL

GREECE TURKEY MALTA CYPRUS

By Raymond Goodburn and
Andrew Houseley

Pilgrim Book Services Limited

© Pilgrim Book Services Limited, Raymond Goodburn and Andrew Houseley
ISBN 978-0-9955615-1-9

Published by Pilgrim Book Services Ltd., registered at 21 Birchwood Drive, Rushmere St Andrew, Ipswich, Suffolk IP5 1EB, United Kingdom.

 www.pilgrimbooks.com

Second Edition 2021

Typesetting and design by Kevin Baverstock.

Cover design by Ivan Yonov; original cover designs by Fielding Design.

Maps by Kevin Baverstock. Data available under the Open Database License. © OpenStreetMap contributors.

Printed in the United Kingdom by Healeys.

MIX
Paper from responsible sources
FSC
www.fsc.org
FSC® C006671

Every effort has been made to contact holders of material which appears in this book. The publishers and author apologise for any errors and omissions.

Cover picture and title page:
St Paul Mosaic of the Altar at the Shrine of St Paul the Apostle, Veria. © Andrew Houseley

CONTENTS

List of Maps & Plans

PREFACE

This book aims to provide information in a concise and portable way. It is a re-write and update of the previous edition, with a little more extensive coverage besides site and city plans, but still does not pretend to be a comprehensive guide to the countries covered. Rather, its purpose is to concentrate on those areas and sites most likely to excite the interest of the Christian visitor. So it is presented as a handy reference book, giving sufficient detail to enable the reader to assimilate easily the relevant data about particular sites, whether read on a plane or coach, hotel room, or as a quick reference while on site. There will be other times for reading more widely and deeply.

Many who read this book will previously have visited the Holy Land. They will, therefore, be familiar with the idea of a pilgrimage or holiday with a purpose and the special benefits gained from travelling with a group of like-minded people. 'Fellowship' can be an over-used word, but its original meaning of 'sharing in the Spirit' is particularly apt for those seeking to follow, for example, in the steps of St Paul. After all, his whole missionary enterprise was prompted and promoted by the Holy Spirit and we who seek to trace something of his journeys do so in that same Spirit. Similarly, St John described himself as being 'in the spirit' when he was challenged to write to the seven churches.

Though the majority of the material in this volume inevitably concentrates on St Paul as the major figure of the early Church, it is only right that St John should also be included as the author of 'The Revelation'. After all, the pilgrim to Turkey will visit some, if not all, of the sites associated with the letters to the seven churches, and those who undertake to explore the lands of St Paul and St John as part of an Aegean cruise will more than likely spend a little time on the delightful island of Patmos, from where 'The Revelation' was written. So the inclusion of a section on Patmos is one of the changes from the previous volume.

This book is offered as some small contribution to appreciating more fully the background to the thrilling story of the growth and development of the early Church in its varied situations. And along the way who knows how our own faith and concern for the mission of the contemporary Church may be enhanced as a result of such journeys? Ours, of course, is a very different world. How, then, do the two worlds relate and how do the insights and understandings of the First century direct our thinking in the 21st?

Ray Goodburn

Christodoulos presents St John the Theologian with the monastery at Patmos

Deesis Mosaic in St Sophia, Istanbul

PART ONE – FROM JERUSALEM TO ROME – THE JOURNEYS

After the Resurrection, the first disciples were directed by the Risen Christ to be witnesses not only in Jerusalem but 'to the ends of the earth.' However, the impetus to turn the vision into reality came from a very unlikely source, one Saul of Tarsus. Commissioned on behalf of Judaism to stamp out this new, upstart religion, little did he know that on just such an assignment to Damascus he, Saul the Christian persecutor, was to undergo a change so dramatic that he was in due course to become Paul, the Christian missionary, the prime agent of fulfilling the post-Resurrection vision.

Much of the story of the Acts of the Apostles deals with the exploits of this remarkable man who, in company with others, took the Christian Gospel from the heart of Judaism in Jerusalem to the centre of the Roman Empire in Rome. Despite hostility, imprisonment, shipwreck, suffering and privation, he single-mindedly adhered to the Damascus Road experience and all that it meant for him as someone appointed to proclaim the Gospel to both Jews and Gentiles. From Jerusalem to Rome, from Jew to Gentile, such became the all-embracing mission of the early Church.

There are three main missionary journeys outlined in Acts. **The first journey** (Acts 13:4–15:4) begins with the selection of Saul and Barnabas for this pioneering work. Starting in Cyprus, the home of Barnabas, it is during his time here that the author of Acts, St Luke, refers to Saul by his Roman name of Paul, the name by which he is known from this point onwards. Sailing from Paphos they journey north to Pamphylia and Pisidia, now known as southern and central Turkey. It is while they are in Perga that John Mark, who has travelled this far with them, decides to return to Jerusalem (Acts 13:13), apparently much to the annoyance of Paul (Acts 15:37ff).

The aftermath of this first journey is the great Council of Jerusalem (Acts 15), called together to debate what requirements, if any, should be laid upon Gentiles who become Christians. Once matters have been resolved, envoys led by Paul and Barnabas are appointed to make the Council's decisions known.

This becomes the springboard for **the second journey** (Acts 15:36–18:22) which, however, begins with Paul and Barnabas parting company over their disagreement about John Mark. Instead, Mark accompanies Barnabas to Cyprus and Silas becomes

Paul's new travelling companion. On their travels through Cilicia, Galatia and Phrygia (modern Turkey), Paul and Silas re-visit some of the churches from their first journey and at Lystra a young man named Timothy becomes another companion. But it is at Troas that the Christian enterprise takes a colossal leap forward. Having received a vision beckoning him to go over into Macedonia, Paul sails there from Troas and, consequently, the Gospel which has taken root in Asia now spreads over into Europe. Landing in Neapolis, he travels a short distance inland to Philippi and so begins a journey through Greece which takes him to the capital of Macedonia, Thessalonika, and then southwards to Athens, the foundation of democracy and the centre of philosophy, literature and art. From here, nearby Corinth becomes his next destination, a cosmopolitan and commercial centre, where Paul stays for some considerable time before returning by way of Ephesus to Antioch-on-the-Orontes, from where he set out.

The end of the second missionary journey more or less runs straight into **the third journey** (Acts 18:23–21:17), so little time does Paul spend in Antioch before setting off again on his travels. He begins in Asia, visiting the churches in Phrygia and Galatia before arriving once more in Ephesus, a journey which must have taken several months. His stay in Ephesus lasts for over two years until a riot by the silversmiths, whose profits seem to have been somewhat eroded by Paul's preaching, signals that it is time to move on. Once more he crosses into Europe from Asia, wanting to strengthen the churches in Macedonia, and spends about three months in Greece, including time in Corinth. Due to a plot by his Jewish enemies he decides not to return to Jerusalem by sailing directly from Greece to Syria, but makes a detour overland to Philippi and sails from here back to Troas. Choosing to go by land from Troas to Assos rather than sail round the promontory, Paul then takes a boat down the west coast of Turkey, arriving in a few days at Miletus where, having summoned the Ephesian elders, he addresses them and takes an emotional farewell. Sailing south via Kos, Rhodes and Patara, Paul and his party transfer to another boat for the journey to Syria, and after landing at Tyre travel to Jerusalem by way of Ptolemais (Acre) and Caesarea.

But his arrival in Jerusalem sparks all kinds of trouble, leading ultimately to his arrest and his appeal as a Roman citizen to present his case to the Emperor. This, in turn, occasions his final journey, the journey to Rome. Imprisoned for some two years in Caesarea, Paul defends himself before two Governors, Felix and Festus, as well as before the King, Agrippa II. Had Paul not appealed to the Emperor then he might well have been released, as the charges against him could not be substantiated – such is the advice of Agrippa to Festus. But having made the appeal, to Rome Paul must go.

A Roman Grain Ship

Under Roman guard he sails first to Myra (Demre) and then to Crete. Against Paul's advice the captain determines to press on with the journey in spite of the worsening weather conditions, typical for the winter period. The result is a terrible storm leading to the shipwreck off Malta, vividly described in Acts 27:13–28:10, and where they are then compelled to spend the winter. Eventually, after three months on the island, they set sail once more and by way of Syracuse, Rhegium and Puteoli, Paul finally arrives in Rome, though presumably not in the way he may previously have imagined.

PART TWO – ST PAUL IN TURKEY

The previous chapter will have illustrated just how important the land of Turkey was in the spread of early Christianity, not only in Asia Minor but also from there as a springboard into Europe. But as already mentioned in the Preface, St John as well as St Paul must also have his due place and this will be done in the next chapter as we look at the letters to the Seven Churches. Furthermore, what also needs to be acknowledged is that between AD 325 and AD 787, Turkey acted as host to seven Ecumenical Councils. The first one, for example, was called by the Emperor Constantine himself and held in the Emperor's Palace in Nicea (AD 325). It was tasked with the responsibility of defining orthodox Christian belief and subsequently produced what is now known as the Nicene Creed. Others dealt with the question of the Person of Christ, 'truly God, truly Man' in one person, particularly the Council of Chalcedon in AD 451. So whilst modern Turkey is secular in government and predominantly Moslem in religion, its Christian past is singularly noteworthy.

A Brief History

Old Testament names such as Noah, whose Ark is believed to have settled on Mount Ararat in Eastern Turkey, and Abraham, whose home was Edessa (modern Urfa), indicate something of the ancient civilization of Anatolia or Asia Minor, as the region was known until more recently. The earliest signs of habitation are believed to go back to Neanderthal times, but evidence for the first settled communities is dated about 6000 BC.

Turkey's subsequent historical development is much too detailed for the scope of a book such as this, but it is important to note particular peoples who created such a rich kaleidoscope of history. The **Persians**, for example, began their dominance of Anatolia in 547 BC when King Croesus was defeated by the Persian, Cyrus the Great (the same Cyrus who freed the Jews from Babylon in 539 BC). A major contribution of this period seems to have been the building of an excellent system of roads.

The area remained under the influence of the Persians for some 200 years until the arrival of Alexander the Great in 334 BC ushered in the **Greek** period. As well as liberating the people of Anatolia, Alexander did much to spread the Greek influence throughout the region, in particular the Greek language and literature. At the same time large new cities were built such as Pergamum and Antioch, with theatres, stadiums and gymnasiums, and most of the ruins which can be seen today stem either from the Greek or Roman periods.

Roman influence began when, in 133 BC, the last King of Pergamum, Attalus III, recognising the increasing power of the Empire in the region, bequeathed his Kingdom to the Romans. From then on began the gradual advance of Rome and the taking over of the various provinces, bringing with it an era of prosperity and political stability. Cities grew both in size and splendour, universities were created, the arts flourished, sport and recreational facilities developed.

During this time thriving Jewish communities established themselves in the cities and it was among these that Christianity found the basis for its rapid expansion throughout the region. As noted in the previous chapter, the agent of this growth was St Paul, a native of Tarsus in southern Anatolia, who travelled the region and beyond during the years AD 45 to 58.

However, as Christianity grew, so too did opposition, and the 2nd and 3rd centuries AD witnessed periodic outbreaks of persecution against the Christians right across the Empire, the most severe during the time of the Emperor Diocletian. All this changed, though, when **Constantine**, who ruled from AD 306 to 337, converted to Christianity. But as well as embracing Christianity he made another decision which was to have a profound effect on Anatolia. He moved his capital from Rome to Byzantium, which he re-named Constantinople, and the **Byzantine Empire** was born, effectively dividing the Roman Empire into east and west, and while the west diminished in influence so the east flourished. Probably the greatest period of Byzantine rule was during the reign of Justinian (AD 527–565), and one of his most notable achievements was the building of the church of St Sophia, dedicated in AD 536, and regarded as the architectural masterpiece of its day.

But from this time onwards the Byzantine influence slowly began to wane (apart from a brief revival in the 9th and 10th centuries) and eventually the importance of Christianity with it. In AD 654 Arab armies coming from the east brought with them the religion of Islam, which was ultimately to become the religion of the country. Even though the writing was on the wall in 1204 when a Fourth Crusade attacked and looted Constantinople, it was not until the May 29th 1453 that the city finally fell, the last bastion of all that remained from the once mighty Byzantine era.

From then until 1923 it was the **Ottoman Empire** which held the ascendancy. Under Sultan Suleyman – popularly known as **Suleyman the Magnificent** – it reached its zenith during the period of his rule (1520–1566). Though the title 'Magnificent' was first given to him by Europeans, his own people regarded him primarily as 'Lawgiver', for a significant

Constantine Directing the Building of
Constantinople (Tapestry, composition by Peter Paul
Rubens): Philadelphia Museum of Art: Gift of the Samuel
H. Kress Foundation, 1959

Suleyman I, the Magnificent
(Master AA, Italian): Philadelphia Museum of
Art: Purchased (by exchange) for the William S.
Pilling Collection, 1945

feature of Ottoman rule was justice for the people. This was an age of major military conquest and expansion, making the Ottoman Empire one of the world's greatest. But as well as being statesman and lawgiver, Suleyman was also credited as a notable patron of the arts and under him the Empire's culture blossomed.

But it was not to last. Though the Empire continued to expand during the early part of the 17th century, the 18th and 19th centuries were a time of steady decline, brought on by pressures from without and conflicts from within. By the end of World War One, when the Turks sided with the Germans, the Empire fell apart. Yet out of this war and in particular the one successful Turkish military action, that of defending the Gallipoli peninsula, there emerged the man who was to transform the nation – **Mustafa Kamal**. On the 29th October 1923 he was elected the first President of the Turkish Republic and took the name **Ataturk** ('Father of the Turks'). His charismatic and determined leadership launched a process of secularisation and westernisation in government, in religion, in education and in dress which was to lay the foundation of modern Turkey.

But since then there have been many ups-and-downs, especially in trying to find political stability and, indeed, between 1960 and the present there have been no less than three coups! Whilst currently the government is looking for EU membership, there have been those who think that the country should look east rather than west for its political and economic partners. In addition, the change since 1923 from a predominantly rural nation to an urban one has put enormous strains on the cities, not least the problems caused by the influx of large numbers of migrants into them. Nor can the influence of Islamic fundamentalism be overlooked in the development of contemporary Turkey.

But none of this should deter the would-be pilgrim from visiting the country and exploring the sites associated with the early growth and development of Christianity in the region. After all, no country the Christian pilgrim visits is going to be without its problems. Those seeking to discover the background both to the mission of the early Church and to the very rich past and present of Turkey, will find that they do so among friendly and hospitable hosts.

WESTERN TURKEY

Beginning in north-western Turkey and progressing steadily south down the Aegean coast to the Mediterranean, **Alexandria Troas** is the starting point for this particular journey. Visited twice by St Paul, it was on the second missionary journey that he here heard the call to take his preaching across the Aegean and into Macedonia (Greece). On the third journey, returning from Macedonia, he stayed in Troas for a week. On this occasion, while Paul was speaking at great length, a young man named Eutychus, who was sitting on a window, fell asleep and tumbled out of the window, landing three floors below. However, when Paul went down to examine him, he was found not to have come to any great harm (Acts 20:5-12).

Once a major port, Troas was founded by one of the generals of Alexander the Great. The site today is much neglected, though the walls of its impressive baths are still on view, and the stadium has recently been revealed. Much of its stonework was transferred from here to help with the building of the new capital, Constantinople.

While in this region it is possible to visit **Troy**, the city of Homer's "Iliad". The stories relating to Achilles, to Helen, to the wooden hose, have all fired the imagination. Indeed, there have been those who considered that ancient Troy might be little more than a creation of Homer's imagination, for by the 6th century AD Troy had been abandoned, its harbour had silted up, and all physical traces had disappeared. All that remained was a hill.

Then, in the 1870s, a German named Heinrich Schliemann began a series of excavations to unearth Homer's Troy, and in the process discovered not just one site for the city but nine, the oldest dating back to about 3600 BC. But still the debate has continued and in particular whether the Trojan War (c.1250 BC) took place as told by Homer.

The entrance to the site is dominated by a modern replica of the famous Wooden Horse, an evocative reminder of the stirring events it is believed to represent. The site itself is something of a mish-mash of the various cities of Troy. The visitor can see, among other things, the particularly impressive, though not extensive walls of Troy VI, the foundations of a bastion, the ruins of the Temple of Athena, the chariot ramp, as well as house foundations, theatres, public bath houses and a sewage system.

Another possible excursion, though again not connected with St Paul, is to **Gallipoli**, which can be reached either by road from Istanbul or by ferry across the Dardanelles from Cannakkale. This was the scene of one of the bloodiest battles of the Great War as British Empire and French forces took the only route for them, by sea through the Dardanelles, in an attempt to re-supply the Russians on the eastern front. But the Turkish army, Germany's ally, stood in the way and after colossal loss of life on both sides, the allies retreated in January 1916. Visits can be made to nearby **Anzac Cove** to see the graves of Australian and New Zealand troops, and to the military museum.

Returning, then, to St Paul. On his third journey, he travelled overland from Troas to **Assos** on the other side of the peninsula. After meeting up with his friends who had undertaken the journey by boat, they then set sail south towards Miletus.

The surrounding area is delightfully rural, giving the impression of a traditional way of life that has changed very little for centuries. As you approach Assos the outline of the **acropolis** can be seen in the distance. A walk up through the village below leads to the top of the hill and the acropolis itself. In its heyday Assos was a centre of learning and teaching for Aristotle, Plato's most famous pupil, lived and taught here for some three years. The citadel is surrounded by walls which stretch for about 2 miles and in places are as high as 14m (46 feet), and set within the citadel is the 6th century BC **Temple of Athena**. All that remains today is the platform of the acropolis and a number of Doric columns. But to stand among the ruins and soak up the wonderful view across the Aegean and the Gulf of Edremit amply repays the uphill walk. While here, there is an opportunity to buy samples of local lace-making and enjoy some refreshment at a local restaurant.

Ephesus

Visited by Paul at the end of his second journey and again on this third, when he stayed here for two years, Ephesus stands unrivalled among the sites of Turkey. At the height of its splendour it was the foremost city of Asia, due to two main features. The first was the harbour, making Ephesus a natural centre for trade throughout the Mediterranean region, so establishing its commercial and banking significance. The second was the

Temple of Artemis/Diana, one of the Seven Wonders of the Ancient World, to which visitors flocked from all over, bringing their gifts for the goddess, a further contributory factor to the wealth and pre-eminence of the city. But the constant threat to its prosperity was the silting up of the harbour and by the 6th century AD this had happened to such a degree that the city was abandoned and a new one created nearby – modern **Selçuk**. Nowadays the sea is some 8km away from Ephesus.

The nearby (25 km) bustling town of **Kuşadasi** is often a base for Ephesus on a land tour and the port for cruise ships. Situated along a gulf, with harbour, bazaar, seafront and several beaches, the resort is popular with international tourists.

Though originally a classical Greek city, most of what is to be seen now dates from the Roman period. There is much to be said for beginning a tour of the site from the second (south) entrance, so allowing a gradual build-up of impact as you eventually approach its most spectacular features.

From the south the route takes you past, among other things, the **East Gymnasium**, the **Odeon**, the **State Agora**, the **Temple of Domition**, dated to the 1st century AD and one of four Temples, and the **Fountain of Trajan**. As the colonnaded road begins to drop downhill, there is a splendid view down to the Library of Celsus at the bottom.

Library of Celsus

Temple of Hadrian

But first, notice the **Temple of Hadrian** on the right, partially restored and particularly attractive. Opposite here is the more recently excavated residential area, where the rich and the powerful lived in their luxurious terraced mansions. Built into the hillside these houses, decorated with mosaics and frescoes, show us something of family life during the Roman period. But please note that there is an additional entrance fee to visit them. Nearby, too, are the public toilets (no, not the modern ones!). Then, as the road turns to the right, there in front of you is the magnificent **Library of Celsus**. A strikingly elegant building, the morning light best helps to bring out its features. Built by Julius Aquila in memory of his father Celsus, whose sarcophagus is in a tomb under the Library, it presents a striking façade of marble adorned with carvings and statues. With a reading room set on three levels, it possessed one of the largest collections of books at that time.

Continuing from the Library along the **Marble Road** in the direction of the harbour brings you to the **Theatre** which, of all the buildings in Ephesus, is the best-known to the pilgrim following Paul. This is where, during his two year stay in the city, a group of silversmiths led by Demetrius caused something of a riot in protest at the preaching of Paul and his companions. As makers of images of Diana, the silversmiths clearly saw that conversions to Christianity were a threat to their work and livelihood. Paul's colleagues,

Gaius and Aristarchus, were dragged into the theatre before the mob, but he himself was restrained from joining them by some of his followers and local officials. Once the trouble had subsided Paul very soon left Ephesus for Macedonia.

Estimated to hold 24 000 people and the largest in Turkey, the theatre was originally of Greek design but then transformed by the Romans. If you can summon up the energy it is well worth the climb to the top seats for a fine view over the city and especially the harbour area. Also, should there be someone in the group with a good speaking voice or even if a group wants to sing, it is a splendid place for experiencing the marvellous acoustic of such buildings.

Leaving the theatre and following the marble-paved and colonnaded road in the harbour direction, brings you to the point where the coach will pick you up if you have begun your visit from the southern end. But before moving on from this site there is one more visit which may be made, and that is to the **Church of St Mary**, a short walk not far from the parking area. A long, narrow building and sometimes described as 'the double church', it may not even have been a church in the first instance. No one seems quite sure about its original usage, maybe a bank and market, but once it was converted into a church it was dedicated to the Virgin Mary and is said to be the first church ever dedicated to her. It was here in AD 431 that the Third Ecumenical Council met.

For the Christian pilgrim there are two further possible visits in the vicinity. One is to the **House of the Virgin Mary**, set in the forested hills near Ephesus, in the village of Meryem Ana. There is a tradition which says that Mary came here with St John and this is where she spent the last years of her life, though there is another tradition that the site of her death is on Mt. Zion in Jerusalem. The house has become an important pilgrimage centre, especially on August 15th to celebrate the Feast of the Assumption. Depending on your tour, the coach may take you here first, before visiting the ruined city; if not on a tour you will need a taxi to take you on a round trip. It is 8.5km from Selçuk, less from the ruins of Ephesus. For more information see: www.hzmeryemanaevi.com/en/worship

The other worthwhile visit is to the **Basilica of St John**, situated towards the foot of the hill on which stands the dominating **fortress of Selçuk**. Built in the 6th century by the Emperor Justinian and now partly reconstructed, it is said to be the burial place of St John, the spot marked by a raised marble slab. The original church was in the shape of a cross, crowned with six domes, and on the site there is a representation of how it probably looked.

If from the vantage point you look towards the main site of Ephesus, you will see

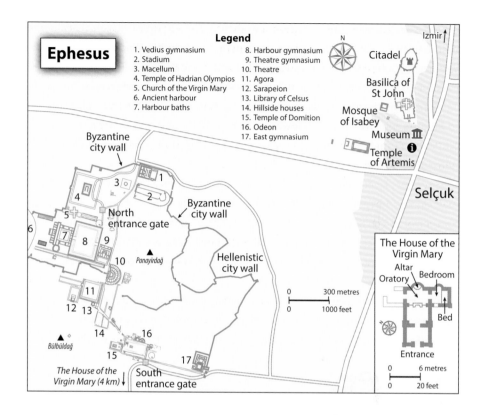

Ephesus

Legend

1. Vedius gymnasium
2. Stadium
3. Macellum
4. Temple of Hadrian Olympios
5. Church of the Virgin Mary
6. Ancient harbour
7. Harbour baths
8. Harbour gymnasium
9. Theatre gymnasium
10. Theatre
11. Agora
12. Sarapeion
13. Library of Celsus
14. Hillside houses
15. Temple of Domition
16. Odeon
17. East gymnasium

N

Izmir ↑

Citadel

Basilica of St John

Mosque of Isabey

Museum 𝍫

Temple of Artemis ❶

Selçuk

Byzantine city wall

Byzantine city wall

North entrance gate

Hellenistic city wall

Panayirdağ

Bülbüldağ

The House of the Virgin Mary (4 km) ↓

South entrance gate

0   300 metres

0   1000 feet

The House of the Virgin Mary

Altar

Oratory

Bedroom

Bed

Entrance

0   6 metres

0   20 feet

below you in a field a single, solitary column, all that remains of the once-wondrous **Temple of Artemis**. First built in the 7th century BC and then replaced in the 6th, it was rebuilt again in the 4th century after having been burned down. A massive structure, some 129.5m (425 ft) long and 68.6m (225 ft) wide, it was constructed predominantly of marble with a wooden roof and surrounded by 127 columns, truly one of the Seven Wonders of the Ancient World. In nearby Selçuk, the **Archaeological Museum** contains two marble statues of Artemis, as well as statues, frescoes, mosaics and coins from Ephesus and deserves a visit.

Some distance inland is all that remains of **Colossae**, overlooking the Lycus valley and once a major city and famous for the dark red wool called 'colossinum'. Destroyed by an earthquake in AD 60, as were Laodicea and Hierapolis, there is very little to be seen today. Paul did not himself visit the city (Col. 1:4), though it had been founded by an assistant of his, Epaphras, who appears to have hailed from here. It was from Epaphras and Onesimus, a runaway slave from Colossae, that Paul heard about its church. Today the site is unexcavated, but discussions between interested parties indicate that at some time in the future archaeological excavations may be possible. When Christian groups visit here it is often linked with visits also to Laodicea and Hierapolis (both mentioned in Col. 4:13). A short climb up the hill gives a good view of surrounding rural Turkey.

Continuing the journey south along the coastal route from Ephesus will bring you to **Miletus**, which Paul visited towards the end of his third missionary journey (Acts 20:15–38). From here he took his emotional farewell of the Ephesian elders before hurrying off to reach Jerusalem in time for Pentecost.

Settlement began here around 1500 BC and in the Greek period it developed as a major Ionian port at the mouth of the Meander River. Though destroyed by the Persian invasion of 494 BC it was quickly rebuilt and in Roman times re-established much of its former prominence. But a great deal of Miletus's fame was based not only on commerce but also on philosophy, being the birthplace of notable philosophers such as Thales, Anaximander and Anaximenes.

On arrival by coach at Miletus the first thing that strikes you is the **Theatre**, set in a hillside and facing the parking area. Of all the remains here it is by far the most grand and, indeed, best preserved. Reconstructed by the Romans it could seat at least 15 000

Miletus   *bySeyyahun/Shutterstock.com*

people. A walk over the hill from the theatre brings you to the city centre, where you will find a **council chamber, nymphaeum**, a 2nd century BC **stadium**, three **market**

places, a **synagogue**, a 5th century AD **church** and a **mosque**. It is also still possible to find the two lions which guarded the entrance to the harbour. But after the theatre, the most well-preserved of all the buildings are the **Baths of Faustina**, dedicated to Faustina, the wife of Marcus Aurelius.

SOUTHERN TURKEY

Journeying further south towards the Mediterranean brings us to **Knidos** (Cnidus). On his final journey to Rome, the captain of Paul's ship intended to land at Cnidus, but the severity of the winds made this impossible (Acts 27:7), so the only claim to Pauline fame was as a landfall rather than a place visited by him. Founded in the 4th century BC and once a flourishing city renowned as a centre of art, many of the finds from here are on display in the British Museum. A stepped street, houses, a theatre and the foundations of the circular temple of Aphrodite can be seen. Though possible to reach by land, it is most accessible by boat.

Following the coastline around towards the east, the next significant place associated with Paul is **Patara**. On the way to Jerusalem from Miletus and towards the end of his first missionary journey, Paul called in here (Acts 21:1). They changed to another ship, possibly a larger one, for the final, longer stage of their journey. But Patara was also the birthplace of Nicholas (c.AD 300), who as well as becoming the first Bishop of Myra, was also at a later stage to be known as St Nicholas (i.e. as Santa Claus).

Once a major port at the mouth of the Xanthus River – and the principal port of Lycia – Patara suffered a similar fate to that of Ephesus, namely, the silting up of its harbour. Alexander the Great and Brutus were both associated with its famous past. Most of the ruins date from Patara's greatest days of the Roman period and fortunately, after centuries of neglect, excavations have begun to rescue its treasures from the invading sands – the **triple-arched gate** (c.AD 100), the large **semi-circular theatre**, the **granary of Hadrian**, **temples**, **baths**, a Byzantine **basilica**, a broad **avenue** leading to the Agora (market place), and even a **lighthouse**. While it can no longer boast about its harbour, it most certainly can about its magnificent sandy beach.

Continuing eastwards we arrive in **Demre** (Kale), site of ancient Myra and the Bishopric of St Nicholas. On his journey to Rome from Caesarea, Paul, along with other prisoners plus some of his friends, stopped off at this important port and changed ships (Acts 27:5–6).

The main point of interest in Demre itself is the **church of St Nicholas**, dating back originally to the 5th century. Used during the earlier part of the 20th century as a

Antalya

substitute for a mosque, the development of tourism enhanced the potential of the church which, after much restoration, was opened in 1981 as a shrine and museum to St Nicholas. Indeed, there are those who associate the origins of Santa Claus with this place in Turkey rather than with snowy locations rather further north! (See also the Archaeological Museum at Antalya). The site of ancient **Myra** is about one mile from the town on the northern outskirts and is noted for two sets of Lycian **tombs** hewn out of the cliffs, as well as a huge Roman **theatre**. Lycian inscriptions and carvings can be seen.

Moving on from here we reach **Antalya**, possibly Turkey's most lovely city set in the most beautiful surroundings and currently the thriving centre of this vastly popular tourist area, an excellent base for visiting either holiday or ancient locations. It was from Antalya (Attalia), then in the region of Pamphylia, that Paul sailed on his way back to Antioch-on-the-Orontes (Acts 14:24–26) at the completion of his first missionary journey.

The town was founded by Attalus II, King of Pergamum, in the 2nd century BC, though an original settlement here is believed to go back to at least 1000 BC. Particularly impressive among the remains on view is **Hadrian's Gate**, a triple-arched marble gate to commemorate the Emperor's visit to the city in AD 130. Also to be seen are **city walls** and **ramparts**, built originally by the Greeks but later restored by the Romans and Selçuks. The **Yivlie Minare** (the 'fluted minaret') is the distinctive symbol of Antalya and the most memorable of all the splendid minarets you are likely to see in Turkey. It was once part of a mosque complex built by the Selçuks in the 13th century and is a fine example of Selçuk craftsmanship. Notice, too, the **Hidirlik Tower**, possibly once a lighthouse and said to contain the tomb of a 2nd century Roman consul.

But before leaving Antalya, pay a visit to the **Archaeological Museum**, displaying exhibits from the Stone Age through to a 6th century AD relief of the Archangel Gabriel.

Perge   *Karavanov_Lev Shutterstock.com*

Greek and Roman sculptures abound, and there is a sarcophagus reputed to hold the remains of St Nicholas of Myra himself.

Almost next door to Antalya is **Perge**, visited by Paul along with Barnabas and John Mark on the first missionary journey (Acts 13:13; 14:25) and, of course, the place where Mark parted company with Paul. Although not as vast as Ephesus and Pergamum, the site of Perge is still particularly impressive. In Hellenistic times it was the principal city of Pamphylia, but it was largely under the Romans that it achieved its greatest prosperity.

Before entering the impressive **double gates** to the city, the visitor will first see the magnificent **theatre** and horse-shoe shaped **stadium**, one of the best preserved in the ancient world. A climb to the top of the theatre furnishes a wonderful view over the city. Inside the city walls are **baths**, a **colonnaded street**, and next to the **agora** are the remains of a Byzantine **basilica**. Further into the city are the **foundations** of the cathedral.

While not all Christian pilgrims following the steps of St Paul will travel much further east along the Mediterranean coast than this, there will be some who do, especially those who want to visit the birthplace of the Apostle, **Tarsus**. Although also associated with the first meeting between Mark Antony and Cleopatra, Tarsus, however, is identified in Christian history with Paul himself. Here he was born a Jew of the tribe of Benjamin, in due course inheriting Roman citizenship and rights from his father, from whom he probably developed his trade as a tent-maker. It was to Tarsus that Barnabas later came to recruit Paul, or Saul as he then was, to share the Christian work in Antioch-on-the-Orontes (Acts 11:25).

Though Tarsus has a rich history, once being a significant Cilician trading port situated on a lagoon, there are very few remains to be observed today which testify to its antiquity, much of which is buried beneath the modern town. There is **Cleopatra's Gate**, dated about 40 BC, and the remains of a 2ⁿᵈ century **Roman temple**. It may be as well not to get too excited about references to 'St Paul's Gate', 'St Paul's Well', or even 'St Paul's House'! But for pilgrims who do venture this far maybe it will be enough just to have visited the location of Paul's birth.

Before leaving this southern Mediterranean coast of Turkey, mention ought to be made of one more Pauline location already referred to, even further to the east and close to the border with Syria – **Antioch-on-the-Orontes**. Set in a delightfully fertile plain and surrounded by hills, Antioch was once the prosperous and flamboyant capital of the Seleucids, whose kings were noted for their flamboyant lifestyles. Founded originally by one of the generals of Alexander the Great, the city flourished during the Hellenistic period, becoming the most significant city of the region, boasting many impressive buildings. It prospered even further under the Romans when it became capital of the province of Syria, establishing itself as a centre of commerce and culture, becoming the third city of the Empire after Rome and Alexandria.

This, then, was the city which served as a base for the work of Peter, Paul and Barnabas. A grotto east of the city and known as the **church of St Peter**, is said to be where Peter first preached and began to consolidate the Christian community in the city. As mentioned previously, it was from here that Barnabas went to Tarsus to enlist Paul's help with the Christian mission in Antioch and it was from here, too, that they set out on their first missionary journey (Acts 13:1–3). It was also in Antioch that the followers of Jesus were first called 'Christians' (Acts 11:26).

CENTRAL TURKEY

This is an area which embraces the remaining sites associated with St Paul, as well as the unique region of Cappadocia, with its amazing landscape and underground cities, a region of compelling allure. But first, let us complete our survey of Paul in Turkey.

Lystra and **Derbe** and are both mentioned during the first missionary journey when Paul and Barnabas, on learning of a plot to stone them in Iconium, fled here (Acts

Mevlana Museum Mosque   *Victor Lauer/Shutterstock.com*

14:1–23). However, having healed a lame man in Lystra, Paul's opponents from Antioch-of-Pisidia and Iconium so influenced the crowds in Lystra, that they stoned him and dragged him out of the city, thinking that he was dead (Acts 14:19-20). Paul and Barnabas then moved on to Derbe where they appear to have received a much more favourable reception and made many converts (Acts 14:21). Today little remains of these sites.

Returning to **Iconium** (Konya), and in spite of opposition, Paul and Barnabas appear to have been reasonably successful, with a great number of Jews and Greeks becoming believers (Acts 14:1) and on the strength of that stayed for some time. Nowadays the city is a centre for both Christian and Moslem pilgrims.

It has a long history, created by Hittites, Phrygians, Lydians, Persians, Greeks and then Romans. But it was during its time as the capital of the Selçuk Empire (1071–1308) that the city experienced a significant cultural renaissance. The beauty of its Selçuk architecture in such buildings as the **Alâeddin Mosque** (with its Roman columns), the **Karatay Medresesi** (a museum of Selçuk and Ottoman ceramics set in a 13th century Selçuk theological seminary), and, of course, the **Mevlana Museum**, which houses the tomb of Mevlana Celaleddin Rumi, founder of the famous 'Whirling Dervishes'. The museum also contains traditional Dervish garments, prayer carpets, and the earliest edition of Mevlana's great poetical and mystical work, The Mesnevi. Accompanied by a reed flute, the whirling of the dancers expresses their search for a mystical union with God.

Antioch-of-Pisidia (Yalvaç) brings us to the final place associated with the travels and preaching of St Paul in Asia Minor. As seen above, his activities here during the first missionary journey as well as creating converts also created dissent (Acts 13:14–52). Originally a Phrygian settlement, the town was founded between 300 and 280 BC and for a long time was the main town of Pisidia. There are the remains of an **arched entrance**, a **temple**, a **church** and a **basilica**, as well as an aqueduct. The **local museum** at Yalvaç houses some of the findings from the site.

This, then, completes our travels with St Paul through Turkey. We can only marvel at the faith and fortitude of a man whose life was so driven by the Damascus Road experience and his missionary zeal, that out of the cradle of Asia Minor there matured a Christian Church whose influence was to become world-wide.

Cappadocia

It can be said without fear of contradiction that there is no place on earth quite like Cappadocia. The unique landscape created by nature over millions of years could almost be something out of a fairy-tale. The origin of this amazing topography is due to volcanic eruption all that time ago, which covered the region with a thick layer of lava and ash called tuff (*tufa*). This in turn, when worked upon by the elements, created a fantastic landscape of valleys along with rocky outcrops sculptured into the most amazing shapes. These outcrops have become known as 'fairy chimneys'. The early inhabitants of the region quickly discovered that the stone is soft until it comes into contact with the air and with this knowledge they were able to carve out their homes from the rock. Much later still, Christians fleeing from Roman and subsequently Arab persecution, created their underground cities, monasteries and churches.

While many Christian pilgrims to Turkey will initially concentrate on Western Turkey, both to explore the Pauline sites and those associated with the Seven Churches, hopefully, if Cappadocia is not part of that initial itinerary, they will want to return and discover this unique region. Though there is no evidence that St Paul visited what is today called 'Cappadocia', it has to be remembered that originally the Hellenistic kingdom and subsequent Roman province of Cappadocia was much more extensive and would certainly have included Iconium (Konya). Once Christianity took root, the region developed into a stronghold of Christian monasticism, with Basil the Great in the 4th century as its dominant figure. As Bishop of Caesarea (now Kayseri) he founded the rules which were the basis of the monastic communities that established themselves in the area.

As there is much more to be seen that the normal tour itinerary will accommodate, what follows concentrates on particular highlights. The capital of the region and an ideal base from which to explore is **Nevşehir** (meaning 'new town'). Though there is not a great deal of antiquity here, as the name of the town implies, it is worth climbing up to the ruined Selçuk castle which affords a splendid viewpoint for the area around. Also take time to visit the **Damad Ibrahim Paşha Mosque**, named after the man who did so much to introduce European art and culture into Turkey.

Travelling further south from Nevşehir we come first to **Kaymakli** and then **Derinkuyu**, two of the best examples of the region's many underground structures. So extensive are these cities that excavations are by no means complete. Several storeys in depth, they were used by Christians seeking to escape from persecution and were capable of accommodating up to 20 000 people. However, the discovery of Roman tombs and what may be a Hittite grain mill suggests that these cities are considerably older. There are churches, living quarters, dining areas, storage rooms and even tombs, all linked by underground tunnels, some as long as six miles, fresh air being supplied by an efficient system of vertical air shafts. The depth of these air shafts, some of 100 metres, gives an idea of the vast scale of some of these cities built storey on storey. The tunnels themselves even contained huge blocking stones by which they could be sealed off quickly in the event of invasion. Marvels of construction, one can only guess at the time-span required to create these labyrinthine cities, but it must have been centuries.

Moving eastwards from Nevşehir brings us to the **Rock of Üçhisar**. One of a number of rock cities in the area it provides an example of how cave dwellings were carved out of the rock face. The climb to the top is recommended for the panoramic view it provides of the Göreme Valley. A few miles further east we arrive at **Göreme** itself and to the **Göreme Valley Museum**, an open-air museum of numerous rock-cut churches dating back to the 10th and 11th centuries, many with beautifully preserved frescoes. This is the largest monastic complex in the area, but even then it represents only a fraction of the 1000 or so rock-cut churches which archaeologists and researches believe exist in the region. Many of them have been sculptured in such a way as to create arches, pillars, domes, as in an ordinary church, but the main difference being that there are no windows. The significance of the paintings is that they portray in art-form the history, beliefs and customs of the people who designed them. Some depict New Testament scenes, others lives of the saints (including St George with his dragon), along with those whose stories are unfamiliar to us.

Göreme National Park   *Travel Faery/Shutterstock.com*

Not far from Göreme, in a northeasterly direction, is **Zelve**, another canyon full of rock churches and in places dense with fairy chimneys. Also, if opportunity permits, do try to visit the **Ihlara Valley**, situated southwesterly from Nevşehir. With its steep-sided red cliffs and fertile green valley, it provides the most dramatic and picturesque of all the settings for the many rock churches, some of which probably date back to the 6th century. Many of these, too, are decorated with excellent frescoes. Needless to say, there are countless rock houses as well.

Though it seems trite to say it, Cappadocia has to be seen to be believed. With its incredible and surrealistic landscape, its underground cities, monasteries, rock churches and paintings, there really is nowhere quite like it, and a visit here cannot be anything less than memorable.

THE SEVEN CHURCHES

Whatever else they do, Christian pilgrims visiting Western Turkey will want to trace not just the steps of St Paul but also the sites of the Seven Churches addressed by the author of the Book of the Revelation. But before we inspect these locations some background on the Book may help to set the scene.

So obscure is the language and imagery of the Book of the Revelation that many Christians are inclined to give up on the unequal struggle and leave it to those for whom it has become a happy-hunting ground of exotic ideas about the future and, indeed, the present. The cause of the Book is not helped by those of its exponents who seek to stamp a literalism on its imagery and poetry that they were never meant to bear. Much of the language of Revelation is that of visionary poetry and any attempt to force a literal interpretation on it does violence to what the author intended. But to those who are prepared to work with the poetry and symbolism and, therefore, grapple with the ideas they represent, then the book comes across as a powerful and original work about Jesus Christ as the final and authoritative revelation of God's purposes for history.

As to who was the author, well that is a challenging question. A little more will be said about that in the chapter on Patmos, from where it is believed the book was written.

A letter to Ephesus (Revelation 2:1–7)

Taking the letters in the order in which they appear in the Book of the Revelation, the first one to consider is to the church in **Ephesus**. It has already been noted that Ephesus was the most significant port in Asia Minor and its most prosperous city, so it is entirely appropriate that the first letter should be to the Christian community here. Each letter has a message specifically addressed to the circumstances of each church and contained within the message is a word of warning relating to that particular situation. The church in Ephesus is praised for the way in which it has withstood heresy from within and persecution from without, but is criticised for losing its early love. Yet as so often in these letters, the negative is followed by a positive word of encouragement (v.7). In terms of Ephesus as an archaeological site, this has been covered previously in pages 15–21.

A letter to Smyrna (Revelation 2:8–11)

Directly north from Ephesus, the courier responsible for delivering these letters would have come to **Smyrna** (modern Izmir). This letter is particularly noteworthy in that it contains no element of blame. The Christians in Smyrna are clearly a struggling community, rich only in their faith, and persecuted by the Jewish community. The warning to the Christians is to remain faithful to death. It is interesting to observe that of all the seven cities, Smyrna is the only one that has survived down the centuries. Among several churches in present-day Izmir, Turkey's third largest city, are the **Anglican Church of St John** and the **Catholic Cathedral of St John the Evangelist**, as well as the **Catholic Church of St Polycarp**. There is still a Jewish community here, though it has declined considerably over the last century.

With a foundation going back to pre-history, which includes Hittite remains, ancient Smyrna eventually developed into a prosperous and beautiful city. This was due mainly to the influence of Alexander the Great in the 4th century BC, who re-sited the city, and later to the Romans. The first Christian congregation would have been drawn from the Jewish community, this in itself being a prime motive for the subsequent persecution. However, by the early part of the 2nd century AD there was clearly a sizeable enough Christian community to support a bishop, the most famous of all being Polycarp, the fourth bishop from 115 to 156, and one of the first Christian martyrs. Arrested and tried by the Roman Governor, Statius Quadratus, Polycarp refused to compromise his allegiance to Christ by acknowledging the sovereignty of the Emperor. 'For eighty and six years I have served Jesus Christ and he has done me no wrong. How can I blaspheme my King?' For his unyielding devotion he was burned at the stake.

Unfortunately, during the evacuation of Greek troops from the region in 1922, a huge, three day fire destroyed much which reflected the history of Izmir. However, not far from the bazaar is one of the most notable remains, the Roman **Agora** (market place). Rebuilt by Marcus Aurelius after the devastating earthquake of AD 178, two rows of colonnades can still be seen, along with statues to Demeter, Poseidon and Artemis. Overlooking the Agora is **Kadifekale**, the Velvet Castle, perched on Mount Pagus and, according to the legend, the place where Alexander the Great was told in a dream to re-site the city and its inhabitants. If there is time, the walk to the top provides wonderful views over the city and bay.

A letter to Pergamum (Revelation 2:12–17)

Although most visitors to Western Turkey will highlight the magnificence of Ephesus, even so **Pergamum** was, and still is, one of the most impressive Classical sites in Turkey. Described by John as the place 'where Satan has his throne', this may be a reference to the temple of Zeus, with its immense altar, or to the power of Rome as embodied in the person of the Roman Governor, who made the city his principal residence. We cannot be sure.

Clearly there had been some local persecution of Christians, yet they had remained faithful. But the real danger to the Christian community seems to have come from the Nicolaitans, also referred to in the letter to Ephesus. Though nothing is known about this group, they were regarded by John as a heretical element within the church and intent on threatening the faithful with compromise of religious and ethical standards. To those who stay constant John promises 'manna'. Just as this manna was the supernatural food which sustained the people of Israel in the wilderness, so it would be the food of the chosen in heaven. The reference to the reward of the white stones is extremely obscure

The Temple of Trajan, Pergamum

but suggests either acquittal or victory.

The site of Pergamum towers over the town of **Bergama**, famous for its rugs and while in the area you may have chance to visit a factory where they are made and even buy the finished product. But be warned – they are hand-made and therefore not cheap. However, if you are more interested in ruins than rugs, then Pergamum itself will enthral you.

It was in the last two centuries BC that Pergamum reached the height of its splendour. During the Greek period it became a principal centre of commerce, culture and medicine and in due course developed into the capital of the Roman Empire in Asia Minor. The journey to the top of its famed **Acropolis** is done by cable car. Once on top you can see the **Upper Agora**, and nearby, somewhat higher up, are the remains of the **Altar of Zeus**, of which only the foundations are visible today. The reconstructed altar can be seen in the Pergamum Museum in Berlin. Most spectacular of all is the **Theatre**, with its 80 rows set into the hillside and with a capacity of 10 000 spectators. If you were seated on the top rows you would need a good head for heights! Mind you, as well as a splendid view of the stage you also have an impressive view of the surrounding countryside. Above the theatre and set on the highest level of the Acropolis is the impressive **Temple**

The Theatre, Pergamum

of Trajan, on which there has been a good deal of restoration. Adjacent to this is the famous **Library**, said to contain 200 000 volumes, making it one of the most famous of libraries, a rival even to that of Alexandria, and alongside the Library is the **Temple of Athena**.

Normal citizens lived further down the hillside and here, as well as the **Lower Agora**, is the **Temple of Demeter**, along with the upper and middle **Gymnasium**, where young men and adolescents trained and studied. In this area, too, are the remains of shops and houses.

But before leaving the region a visit to the nearby **Asclepion** is much recommended. Dedicated to Asclepios, the god of Medicine, this was a kind of health spa in which, for example, an over-wrought businessman, politician or whoever, could come to be 'de-stressed'. Such a person would be led down the colonnaded Sacred Way and offered a choice of facilities to aid the healing process. On offer was psychotherapy, a library with good books, a theatre, and the opportunity for a dip in the sacred waters, which were thought to be a significant part of the healing process.

A letter to Thyatira (Revelation 2:18–29)

Apart from here there is only one other mention of **Thyatira** in the New Testament and that is during Paul's second missionary journey when he visited Philippi in Macedonia and there met Lydia, a woman who was selling expensive purple cloth (Acts 16:14). As with the letter to Pergamum, John begins by praising the record of the Christians in Thyatira, but like Pergamum they are threatened from within. The strong language of the letter warns the congregation that they are in serious danger of being led astray by a heretical group, who were wanting to lead them into pagan ways. But as with the other letters this one ends with a promise that those who stand firm against the heresy and who are victorious will share in the sovereignty of Christ.

There is nothing especially impressive about Thyatira's history, though in Hellenistic times it was a garrison of supreme importance for Greek soldiers. Subsequently, when it became part of Rome, industry and commerce seem to have been the main features, with a particular emphasis on making the royal purple cloth. Trade guilds were also very strong. What remains of the ancient town is to be found in the centre of modern **Akhisar**. There is part of a colonnaded street, a temple, and walls of a church.

A letter to Sardis (Revelation 3:1–6)

Once the capital of the Lydian kingdom, **Sardis** was a centre of wealth and influence during the reign of Croesus – the last of its kings (560 to 546 BC). A hub of commercial life in the western Mediterranean, much of its wealth was in gold washed down from the mountain by the river Pactolus. Whilst its importance remained undiminished well into the first century BC, an earthquake in AD 17 destroyed most of the city. Though it was rebuilt by the Emperor Tiberius and was to become a centre of Christianity with an eminent bishopric, it never fully regained its previous glory.

Maybe John, in writing his letter to Sardis, was drawing a parallel between the waning influence of the city and the declining enthusiasm of its Christian community. The church is living on its past reputation and rather than being alive it is now dead. Yet, there is still a nucleus who have remained faithful and they will wear the white robes of those who will be admitted to heaven. This, too, is the promise held out to the rest of the Christian community if they wake up and once more begin to live faithfully in the way of Christ.

To the modern visitor, one of the most immediately obvious and, indeed, impressive features of the site is the **Roman gymnasium** and **baths** dating back to the 2nd century

AD. Situated just off the main road, what is seen today is a major reconstruction of the complex. The magnificent entrance to the gymnasium is through columns decorated with the heads of gods. Adjacent to here are the reconstructed remains of a huge **synagogue**, testifying to the size and influence of the Jewish community. Notice the colourful floor mosaics made from small pieces of marble. Alongside the synagogue is a row of shops with varying trades identified.

While many tour itineraries may not have time for further exploration, there is, however, more to be seen on the opposite side of the road. The **House of Bronzes** takes its name from the many pieces of bronze found here, and given their religious character it is possible this may have been the residence of the Bishop of Sardis. But if the gymnasium-bath complex is the most immediately impressive site to the visitor, the **Temple of Artemis** is undoubtedly its most spectacular. Vast in size it measures 100m by 50m (329ft x 165ft) and particularly splendid are its two remaining beautiful Ionic capitals. Visitors with the time, or maybe the energy, to walk up to the **acropolis**, will find a magnificent panoramic view is the reward for making the effort.

A letter to Philadelphia (Revelation 3:7–13)

On reading this letter it is noticeable that there is no real note of criticism directed at this Christian congregation. The whole tone of the message has a much more gentle character. The church appears to be one of the least distinguished, with little power. Such criticism as it does contain is directed again, as at Sardis, to the members of Satan's synagogue. The Christians are reminded that they have an immense missionary task before them and are promised that for their constancy and endurance they will be pillars in God's temple, in other words, their salvation is guaranteed.

Philadelphia was founded by Attalus II in the 2nd century BC. The town took its name from the fact that Attalus was called *philadelphus*, 'loyal brother', by Eumenes his brother, who was King of Pergamum before him. Like most towns in the vicinity, Philadelphia suffered from major earthquakes, especially during the reign of Tiberius (AD 14–37), one of the most severe being in AD 17. Little of note is left from the ancient town, though the remaining massive pillars of the church of St John reflect its Christian past.

A letter to Laodicea (Revelation 3:14–22)

Whereas the church at Philadelphia was the recipient of unstinting praise, so the church at **Laodicea** received unmitigated criticism. Not far from either Colossae or Hierapolis, Laodicea was famed for its wealth, its textile trade, and its medical school. But such was

Laodicea   *Poliorketes/Shutterstock.com*

the church's compromise with the secular spirit of the time, that it had lost hold of its Christian values. Neither hot like the nearby springs of Hierapolis (Pamukkale), nor cold like refreshing spring water, the Christians at Laodicea were lukewarm, and the only value of such water was to make one vomit! But in spite of the harsh criticism, along with the judgement there is also the promise of a new way forward from the One who stands at the door and knocks.

Built during the 3rd century BC, the city was named after Laodice, wife of Antiochus II, its founder. Until quite recently it had received little attention from archaeologists, but latterly extensive excavations and reconstruction have been undertaken, revealing a city some two miles square. Situated near the Lycus river, it was located on major trading routes running east-west and north-south, and this helped to establish its reputation as a commercial centre. It also became an important bishopric. The ongoing exciting excavations are doing much to unearth its history. Among the discoveries are **theatres, bath complexes, temples, fountains, burial grounds, streets and shops flanked by colonnades**, as well as **churches** (one believed to from the 4th century). Clearly these are momentous times in the emergence of Laodicea, which is rapidly becoming a 'must see' for pilgrims and tourists. Whether, as some think, it will become a major attraction on a par with Ephesus only time will tell.

Though not one of the seven churches, nearby **Hierapolis** (Pamukkale) is usually on the itinerary of most organised tours. Meaning 'Cotton Castle', Pamukkale is probably the best known and most visited of all the hot springs in Turkey. The calcium-laden waters have formed a remarkable white cascade stretching down the hillside, a great attraction drawing many visitors. Yet, for the Christian pilgrim Hierapolis is no less significant. Indeed, in Colossians 4:13, St Paul refers to Epaphras working hard for the Christians in Colossae, Laodicea and Hierapolis.

Dating back to the 2nd century, Hierapolis is associated with the Apostle Philip, whose Martyrium has been discovered here. Also on site is an extensive **cemetery**, said to contain more than a thousand tombs and the subject of continuing excavations, a **Basilical church**, a ceremonial **triple-arched gate**, the **temple of Apollo**, and alongside this the **Ploutonion**, a shrine honouring the god of the underworld. Further up on the hill is a well-preserved **Roman theatre**, and further on still is the **Martyrium** itself, with the tomb claimed to have been discovered in 2011. The saint's relics are in the Santi XII Apostoli Basilica in Rome.

ISTANBUL

For most visitors to Western Turkey some time spent in Istanbul will be regarded as a 'must'. Though, of course, not having any direct association with St Paul himself, Istanbul, nonetheless, is an amazing city with a fascinating blend of European and Asian cultures and styles. No visit here is likely to be a disappointment.

Strategically positioned on the Bosphorus and previously known as Byzantium, it was not until Constantine the Great built his new capital on the site and had it re-named Constantinople in AD 330, that full advantage of its splendid location was taken. Though the original intention was to construct the new capital at Troy on the Dardanelles, a change of mind sent the Emperor in the direction of Byzantium. However, in creating Constantinople his aim was not just to build a magnificent city rivalling the splendours of Rome, but also to establish it as a Christian capital city for the new Christian Empire.

Constantinople soon developed into the great metropolis of the eastern empire – and the Byzantine era continued to flourish – reaching its zenith as a city of great magnitude and opulence during the time of Justinian (AD 527–565). The Byzantine Empire lasted for nearly a thousand years more, but increasingly became a shadow of its early glories. The arrival of the Ottoman Empire in the 15th century heralded the final eclipse of Constantinople and the Empire that went with it. Under the Turks, Istanbul

Istanbul and the Bosphorus

was born.

But the city today is not just a monument to its rich and varied past, though there is plenty to mark that history. Istanbul is very much a vibrant, developing modern city, which amply repays time spent there.

Obviously the Christian pilgrim will want to seek out some of the specific sites associated with Christianity. However, with the exception of one Byzantine church, at some stage all the others were converted into mosques, as is the case with one of Istanbul's great show pieces, **St Sophia** (or, **Hagia / Aya Sophia**), a place which is sacred to both Christians and Moslems. It represents a crossroad between Europe and Asia, Christianity and Islam. One of the greatest examples of Byzantine architecture, the present building is the third to be erected on this site. The first church was built in AD 360 during the time of Constantinus, the son of Constantine, but it was destroyed by fire in AD 404. Its successor in AD 415 was again destroyed by fire in AD 532. The present Justinian basilica was begun shortly after, and when completed in AD 537 was regarded as a marvel of its time. Nothing like it had ever been attempted previously or even envisaged. It remained a Christian church until the Turkish occupation in the 15th century, when it was transformed into a mosque. In 1935, it became a museum, and now in 2020, the much more recent speculation about it returning to a mosque

has been realised.

The vastness of the nave, plus the size and height of the dome, are strikingly impressive as, too, are the mosaics, though some of them are very dimly lit. For example, above the main doorway is a mosaic depicting Jesus, Mary and the Archangel Gabriel, and in the apse above where the altar would have stood is one of Mary and the infant Jesus. Some of the most easily viewable mosaics are in the upper galleries, such as the one portraying Jesus, Mary and John the Baptist and dated the 14th century. Indeed, the mosaics on view today date mostly from the 9th century onwards. In recent years an ongoing programme of restoration has done much to preserve St Sophia.

The one Byzantine church which has never been converted to a mosque is that of St Irene ('Divine Peace'). Not far from St Sophia it stands in the grounds of the Topkapi Palace. Believed to be Constantine's first Cathedral until the building of St Sophia, St Irene was the venue for the meetings of the Second Ecumenical Council in AD 381. During the Ottoman period the building served as an arsenal, and these days is open to the public as a museum, and has served as a venue for the Istanbul Music Festival.

Staying with the Byzantine theme, a visit to the **Byzantine** or **Basilica Cisterns** is highly recommended. Diagonally across from St Sophia and built by Justinian in AD 532 to house the imperial water supply, the 336 marble columns in these underground

Inside Hagia Sophia

cisterns give you the impression of being in a huge Basilica. With piped classical music and atmospheric lighting, a walk around the cisterns is one of the highlights of a visit to Istanbul.

In terms of religious buildings, the **Blue Mosque** should not be missed by any visitor. Situated opposite St Sophia, it was built for Sultan Ahmet I between 1609 and 1617. With its domes, six minarets (the only mosque to have this number) and 260 windows, it is indeed impressive. But most striking of all is the interior, decorated with many thousands of blue Iznik tiles and it is from these that it takes its popular name.

However, perhaps even more elegant and splendid is the **Mosque of Suleyman the Magnificent**. Constructed between 1550 and 1557, it stands majestically on a hill, dominating the skyline of the **Golden Horn's** (Haliç - the major inlet of the Bosphorus) west bank. With four gracefully slender minarets at each corner of the courtyard, the mosque is a model of proportion and perfection. Everything about it from its columns, arches and stained glass windows gives the impression of being just right. There are those who recommend that if you have time to visit only one of the imperial mosques in Istanbul, this should be the one.

Equally demanding of the visitor's time is the **Topkapi Palace**. Such are the treasures on view, that for those who are especially interested a whole day could be spent here. Once the home of the Ottoman rulers, the Palace is built round a series of courtyards. On entering through the main, stone gate, the visitor is inside the first courtyard, a park-like area, and it is here on the left that the church of St Irene can be seen. At the end of the first courtyard is another gateway, where you buy your tickets, and once through here you are in the main body of the Palace.

The second courtyard contains on one side, the **Harem**, which consists of a group of buildings and courtyards where the wives and concubines of the sultans lived separated from the rest of the Palace, and on the other side, the **Palace Kitchens**. On display is a wonderful collection of silver and priceless Chinese porcelain.

The third courtyard houses an exhibition of the various **treasures** of the sultans, with vessels and weapons adorned with the most fabulous jewels. Here is the famous Emerald Dagger as featured in the film 'Topkapi', but even this is no match for the stunning 86-carat Spoon Diamond. So magnificent is this display of gems that it is almost overpowering as you walk through the four rooms, taking in splendour after splendour. Also in this section of the Palace can be seen the various robes worn by the sultans and their families, and in another part of the courtyard is the **Pavilion of the Holy Mantle**, said to preserve various relics of the Prophet Mohammed.

The Blue Mosque

Beyond this fourth courtyard is an outer one which houses the **Archaeology Museum**, containing one of the most famous of all sarcophogi, the Alexander sarcophagus, depicting various scenes from his life and regarded as a particularly fine example of late Roman sculpture. In addition there are bronze pedestals, coats of arms, Greek and Roman bronzes, as well as impressive Trojan jewellery. The other buildings accommodate the **Museum of the Ancient Orient**, with finds from Turkey and the Middle East, and the Tiled Kiosk, with a fine display of Turkish ceramics. The outer part of the Palace provides magnificent views over the Sea of Marmara and the Bosphorus. There is also a very good restaurant!

A book such as this can only pick out some of Istanbul's highlights. Depending on

The Imperial Hall, Harem, Topkapi Palace   Ruslan Kalnitsky/shutterstock.com

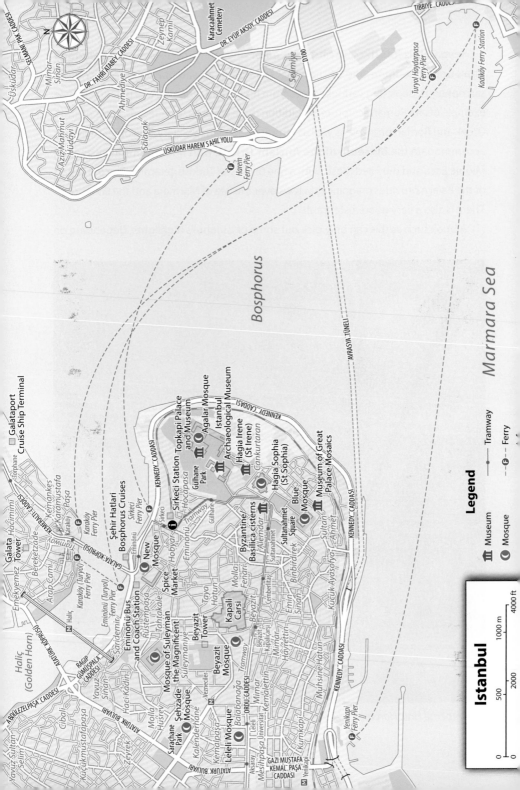

Istanbul

Legend

🏛 Museum   —— Tramway

◯ Mosque   --Ⓕ-- Ferry

Scale: 0 — 500 — 1000 m — 2000 — 4000 ft

Bosphorus

Marmara Sea

Üsküdar

Haliç (Golden Horn)

Galata Tower

Galataport Cruise Ship Terminal

Şehir Hatları Bosphorus Cruises

New Mosque

Spice Market

Sirkeci Station

Topkapi Palace and Museum

Agalar Mosque

Istanbul Archaeological Museum

Gülhane Park

Hagia Irene (St Irene)

Hagia Sophia (St Sophia)

Blue Mosque

Museum of Great Palace Mosaics

Byzantine/Basilica cisterns

Sultanahmet Square

Kapali Carsi

Beyazit Tower

Beyazit Mosque

Mosque of Suleyman the Magnificent

Sehzade Mosque

Sarachane Park

Leleli Mosque

Eminönü Bus and Coach Station

Karaahmet Cemetery

Harem Ferry Pier

Turyol Haydarpaşa Ferry Pier

Kadıköy Ferry Station

Yenikapi Ferry Pier

Karaköy Ferry Pier

Karaköy (Turyol) Ferry Pier

Eminönü (Turyol) Ferry Pier

Sirkeci Ferry Pier

Kapali Carsi

how long you stay here, highly recommended is a **cruise** on the Bosphorus, whose waters divide Asia from Europe. Visits to the **Spice Market** and the famous **Kapali Carsi** or Covered Market should not be missed. This latter is the largest Oriental market in the world, a labyrinth of streets and shops, where you can try your skill at haggling! Whether your interest is a piece of jewellery, decorated pottery, leather goods or leather clothing, or some simple souvenir of your visit to Istanbul, you are sure to find it here.

For more information on Istanbul's museums visit: https://muze.gen.tr

PART THREE – ST PAUL IN GREECE

For many contemporary visitors to Greece it is the islands rather than the mainland which is the prime attraction for sun, sand and sailing. However, for the Christian pilgrim, it is the mainland which is the principal inducement.

As noted in Part 1, it was while Paul was in Troas on his second missionary journey that he received the vision beckoning him to go over to Macedonia (Acts 16:8–10). By responding in the way he did, Paul expanded the range of the gospel from Asia Minor into Europe and eventually of course, into the heart of the Empire, Rome.

HISTORICAL BACKGROUND

Greece's history is long and varied, from the Minoan civilization around 3000 BC, through Philip of Macedon and Alexander the Great, the Roman Empire, the Byzantine era, the Ottoman Empire, to the War of Independence in 1821 and ultimately to membership of the European Union in 1981. With such a richly accumulated past it seems invidious to select one particular period which marked the zenith of Greek civilization, but such a choice would undoubtedly be the Classical period. This was the great era of art, writing and philosophy, with names such as Aeschylus and Euripides, Herodotus and Thucydides, Socrates and Plato. During this period, too, the Parthenon was built, the Peloponnesian War between Athens and Sparta occurred, and the Oracle of Apollo at Delphi experienced its heyday in influencing political decisions. Along with much creativity there was also much upheaval. But the rise to power of Philip of Macedon in 359 BC brought the Classical period to an end. If quality was the hallmark of Classical Greece, it was quantity which most characteristically defined the Hellenistic period with the rapid expansion of the Greek-speaking world, particularly under Philip's son, Alexander the Great.

Though aged only 20 when he succeeded his father, Alexander possessed a driving ambition and a determined ruthlessness. So colossal were his triumphs that the Persians were defeated and a vast Empire established. He was undoubtedly the major figure of this period of Greek history. Even though he died in 323 BC at the early age of 33, his achievements belied the brevity of his life. Despite the fact that there was no one of comparable stature to follow him, the Hellenistic era continued to thrive until the advent

Philip   *Alexander*

of the Romans at the beginning of the 2nd century BC.

Although Greece was regarded by the Romans as a centre of culture and learning with Athens notably as its focal point, it was, however, a time of general decline in prosperity. Nonetheless on the plus side, the influence of Rome specifically during the reign of Augustus, brought a much-needed time of peace and stability. Then, with the coming of Constantine the Great and the founding of the new eastern capital of Constantinople, the Roman Empire divided into the Latin-speaking west and the Greek-speaking east. With the dawn of the Byzantine Empire, which took over from the old eastern Roman Empire and continued until 1453 when Constantinople was captured by the Ottomans, Greece became associated with Byzantine east. For most of this period the country was little more than a backwater and Athens a city of minimal influence.

Until the declaration of independence and start of conflict on March 25th 1821, the Greek state as such was in eclipse. Ruled by the Turks, the Orthodox Church was given an administrative responsibility for overseeing the Christian part of the population, for in the main the sultans regarded the Church as a useful vehicle for implementing Turkish law within the Christian community. This in turn gave the Church the opportunity to maintain the Greek identity through the survival of its culture and language.

But with the outbreak of the War of Independence, Greece was eventually to establish itself, in the modern sense, as an independent nation. Not that that solved everything. Many Greeks were dissatisfied with the slow progress towards prosperity, and political intrigue and in-fighting blighted its development. In truth, it was not until 1832 that Greece was finally declared an independent kingdom. One way or another conflict was to be the nation's continuing story, whether World War One, or the disastrous attempt to conquer Constantinople in 1922, or occupation by the Germans, Italians and Bulgarians in World War Two, or the Civil War of 1946–1949, or the military junta imposed by the Greek Colonels from 1967–1974. This is without mentioning the Cyprus problem during the 1950s and still a matter of issue between Greece and Turkey. Nowadays Greece is a democracy and a member of the European Union, but in 1981 even that decision was the cause of major division within the country. And, of course, the subsequent need for a series of bailouts from the Eurozone and IMF occasioned further political unrest.

But with spectacular scenery, wonderful weather, generous hospitality and magnificent Christian and Classical sites, the Greece of today has much to inform and inspire the Christian pilgrim. Those seeking to follow the steps of St Paul in this country of many contrasts and delights will surely not be disappointed.

A good way of organising a land tour is to fly into Thessalonika in the north and fly out from Athens further south. This section of the book, therefore, begins in the north with Thessalonika and its associated sites, and then journeys south via the Meteora monasteries and Delphi. If time is short it is possible to travel directly from Thessalonika to Athens, but should time not be a premium, it is highly recommended to visit the amazing area of the monasteries and then Delphi, before finally arriving in Athens. A Cruise itinerary should also be able to accommodate most of the sites described here, although a sail along the Corinth Canal may require changing to a smaller craft.

THESSALONIKA

For the Christian pilgrim, Thessalonika provides an excellent centre for visiting not only the city itself, but also some of the other significant Pauline locations in the area, such as Philippi, Kavala (ancient Neapolis) and Beroea (Veria), along with the important Macedonian sites of Pella and Vergina. So, let us start with **Thessalonika** and then move outwards to other places.

In antiquity it was the capital of the Roman Province of Macedonia and is today the second city of the country. Founded in 315 BC by the Macedonian King, Cassander, and named after his wife, the city stood on the Via Egnatia, a major imperial route across northern Greece which linked Rome in the west with the Adriatic in the east. A thriving seaport, Thessalonika was a city of considerable importance and prosperity, and within it contained a notable Jewish community and synagogue. So it was a natural centre for St Paul, accompanied by Silas, to visit on his second missionary journey.

His time in the region is described in Acts 16:11–17:14, beginning with the landing at Neapolis and ending with the departure from Beroea for Athens. This was in response to the vision in Troas where Paul believed he was being called to cross over from Asia Minor into Macedonia, the 'Macedonian Call', and in doing so to begin establishing Christianity in Europe.

The account of Paul's stay in Thessalonika as recorded in Acts is clearly a much-telescoped one, giving the impression that he may have been here only a very short time, whereas in reality it was probably a stay of several months. Indeed, from what he himself writes in his first letter to the Christians here, it appears that he stayed long enough to establish a church of quite some importance (I Thess. 1:6-10) and during that time performed manual work in order to sustain himself and not be a burden on the local folk (2 Thess. 3:8). Furthermore, he also received financial support from the Christians in Philippi (Phil. 4:16). Whatever the complete details of his stay in the city, it is clear that he began with his usual strategy of preaching to the Jews. Though there was some success among them, it was the enthusiastic response of the Gentiles which provoked jealousy among the Jews and this in turn led to Paul and Silas moving on from Thessalonika to Beroea. Not long after his visit to the city, Paul wrote his first letter to the church there, probably about AD 50 or 51 from Corinth, so making it the earliest of his surviving letters and, furthermore, the earliest of any New Testament writing.

Though it is very difficult to pinpoint with any certainty particular sites in Thessalonika which may have been directly associated with St Paul, as most of the ancient city lies beneath the modern one, there is still more than enough to satisfy the particular interest of the Christian pilgrim. There is one possible link, but no more than that, and it is the beautiful little **Monastery of Vlatadon**, founded in the 14th century, and by tradition said to have been built on the site where the Apostle preached on his second missionary journey and from where he and Silas escaped from the city during the night.

Other churches abound, with the richest collection of Byzantine churches anywhere in Greece, including the largest anywhere in the country, **Agios Dimitrios**. Built

Monastery of Vlatadon

originally in about AD 313, it was rebuilt after a fire in the 7th century, and again in the 20th, though on a fifth century plan, after the great fire of 1917. It celebrates the patron saint of Thessalonika, Dimitrios, who as a young man joined the Roman army but also converted to Christianity. However, when ordered to renounce his beliefs he refused and on the instruction of the Emperor Galerius, an infamous and ruthless persecutor of Christians, he was duly executed in AD 305. The crypt is believed to be the oldest surviving part of the church and marks the place where Dimitrios was put to death. In spite of past damage and the need for rebuilding, there are some remaining mosaics probably from the early 7th century, and not surprisingly Dimitrios features in a number of them.

Nor should you miss the church of **Agia Sofia**, and people who have visited Istanbul will find it a reminder of the one-time church become mosque there. Only, in Thessalonika's case, what was built as a church in the mid 8th century and became a mosque in the 16th, reverted to being a church in the 20th. Though somewhat stark in appearance from the outside, the interior is much more striking with mosaics and frescoes dating back to the 9th and 10th centuries. The most impressive of these is a large, well preserved mosaic depicting the Ascension and set in a 30 metre high dome.

Yet another church worth seeking out is that of **Osios David**, a comparatively small, 5th century chapel which was once part of a large monastery. Behind the altar is

The White Tower

a particularly fine mosaic representing the Vision of Ezekiel and which contains an unusual portrayal of a youthful Christ without a beard. There are other mosaics dating from the 12th century.

If there is time and inclination there are, of course, other churches deserving a visit, for example, the churches of **Agioi Apostoloi** and **Nikolaos Orfanos**. Both have fine examples of religious art with some beautiful mosaics and frescoes. On the other hand, the Christian visitor following the steps of St Paul through Greece is likely to have limited time and in addition will want to see other things in Thessalonika.

An absolute priority must be the **Archaeological Museum** which was opened in 1963. Here you can view Prehistoric, Macedonian, Roman and Hellenistic finds from the area around. On display are sculptures, glittering jewellery, silver drinking cups and ivory miniatures. While many of the treasures belonging to King Philip II of Macedon, the father of Alexander the Great, have been relocated to a special museum at the royal tombs at Vergina, there remains a remarkable collection of ancient discoveries and most definitely not to be omitted from any itinerary.

For those who are interested, situated just behind the Archaeological Museum is the **Museum of Byzantine Culture**, opened in 1995, with displays of Byzantine icons from the 15th to the 19th centuries, and there is also some splendid jewellery. Another fascinating visit may be made to the **Folklore and Ethnological Museum**, with exhibits from the last 250 years of Greece's national history. There are weapons, household utensils, national costumes and jewellery, plus accounts of rural and religious festivals, along with a photographic portrait of Thessalonika in the early 20th century.

One further location which most visitors will want to explore is the **White Tower**, probably Thessalonika's most famous landmark. No longer white in colour, it appears to have taken that description from an infamous event in 1826 when mutinous Janissaries, the Sultan's guard, were massacred. In consequence it became known as the 'Bloody Tower', though when the resulting evidence of the massacre was whitewashed out, it took its current name. The several floors and small circular rooms of the museum contain an exhibition of coins, pottery, mosaics, fragments of frescoes, column capitals, ritual burial offerings and ecclesiastical objects, all covering the period from about AD 300 to 1430. The spiral stairs around the rooms lead up to the roof, which affords a fine view over the city and the Theramic Gulf.

MACEDONIA
Eastern Macedonia

Southeast of Thessalonika lies the region of **Halkidiki**, a peninsula consisting of three finger-like peninsulas jutting out into the Aegean Sea. A region of hills, valleys, trees and beaches, it is a popular holiday area. One of its most distinguished features, however, situated at the most southern end of the most easterly peninsula, is **Mount Athos**, a collection of monasteries some of which date back to the 10th century. For more than 1000 years a community of monks has lived the daily life and practices of the Byzantines. At the moment there are about 20 monasteries functioning, and anyone fortunate enough to visit will be impressed by the frescoes and mosaics, the rich libraries and the precious art miniatures. That said, it is not easy to gain access to the monasteries and, indeed, women are strictly forbidden. A view from a boat trip round the peninsula is the nearest most people will get.

In general, itineraries may not have time to include even the sail around Mount Athos and will concentrate on driving eastwards across the northern part of the region along by the sea and beaches to **Kavala**, founded in the 6th century BC and identified with the port of Neapolis as the first place in Europe on which St Paul set foot. Today it is a bustling city built around its **harbour**, though originally it was the port which served nearby Philippi. For the Christian pilgrim on a day excursion to Philippi from Thessalonika, Kavala may be little more than a coffee or lunch-stop, but a very pleasant place in which to experience either. There are currently no reminders of Paul's landing here, but if there is time to wander round, the 16th century Turkish **aqueduct** should not be missed. Venturing up the promontory above the harbour to the **old town** and its castle reveals more history. The **Archaeological Museum** contains finds from Neapolis, Amphipolis and the wider region.

A short drive inland is **Philippi**, named by Philip II. One of its claims to fame is that of being the scene, in 42 BC, of a great battle between the forces of Brutus and Cassius – both of whom had taken part in the assassination of Julius Caesar two years previously – and those of Antony and Octavian, whose armies were victorious in the engagement.

Philippi

By the time St Paul visited Philippi (Acts 16:11–40) it had become thoroughly Romanised and, as the first main stop on the Egnatian Way from Asia to the Adriatic, had developed into an important city.

The conversion of Lydia, from Thyatira in Asia Minor and a seller of its luxurious purple cloth, enabled the missionaries to establish a base in Philippi due to the hospitality she provided for them. Paul's own letter to the church here, written some time later, indicates that he founded a thriving Christian community. As already noted, the church was most generous in the financial support it contributed to the apostle during his stay in Thessalonika. Indeed, the letter he wrote to the Philippians conveys the warmth he felt for them.

The visit of Paul and Silas to the city is also notable for the exorcism of a slave girl, which led to the apostles being beaten and imprisoned, but then eventually escaping during an earthquake, an event seen as miraculous, leading as it did to the conversion and baptism of the jailer and his family. This became the spur for the apostles to move on, but not without an apology from the local magistrates who had broken the law by beating Roman citizens.

The ruins at Philippi are extensive. On one side of the road lie the remains of a 5th century **church** with aisles, transepts and a semi-circular apse. Near here also is said to be the prison where Paul and Silas were held. Before leaving the ruins on this side of the road there is also the **Theatre**, originally of Greek design but later re-styled to suit the Romans. The majority of what can be seen today is a reconstruction, with just a few original Roman tiers.

Crossing the road brings you to the main and indeed, more interesting part of the site. Here is the **Forum**, dating back to the time of Marcus Aurelius. Though the remains do not reach any great height, the fertile imagination can soon build up a picture, using the foundations of two temples and a library. Note too, the great size of many of the stones and slabs. Presumably it was here that St Paul did some of his preaching. But the most impressive remains are those of another **Basilica** built during the reign of Justinian (AD 527–565). This was intended to be an architectural masterpiece, a great domed church, but during the construction the dome above the sanctuary collapsed and the building was never completed. But there is more than enough still available to interest the visitor, with piers, columns and sculptured decorations. Also to be seen on the site is a large number of marble seats which constituted the public toilets! In addition you

Shrine at Lydia   *The Lion of Amphipolis*

55

can walk on a stretch of the ancient Egnatian Way, built in the first part of the 2nd century BC, so making it easier to move troops from Rome throughout the Empire.

Before leaving the area a short drive is recommended to see a **shrine** beside a river commemorating the baptism of **Lydia**, in a village of the same name. Steps lead down to the simple spot of tradition, with a more elaborate modern baptistery church alongside.

On the way back to Thessalonika, a small detour brings you to the **Lion of Amphipolis**. This enormous statue of a lion, with a splendid mane and glaring eyes, was re-assembled from 4th century fragments and guards the mouth of the river Strymon. A magnificent representation of a lion, it was more than probably seen by St Paul as he passed through Amphipolis on this way from Philippi to Thessalonika. The city and port of Amphipolis was where Alexander the Great prepared for his eastern conquests, along with his generals and admirals. The excavations to date – including a huge tomb, remains of an ancient wooden bridge, and museum – await the visitor with more time to explore the area.

Western Macedonia

If necessary, the main sites in this area can be covered in one long day tour – Pella, Edessa, Veria and Vergina. The only site associated with St Paul is **Veria** – New Testament Beroea (Acts 17:10–14). Lying south of the Via Egnatia it possessed a flourishing Jewish community, among whom Paul found a more ready and receptive audience than in Thessalonika. Gentiles too, along with Jews, responded eagerly to the Christian message and many became believers. It was only when Jews from Thessalonika, hearing of what was happening in Beroea, came there to incite trouble, that the Apostle was encouraged by the new believers to move on.

Here, too, there is no site directly associated with Paul's visit. There are remains of Roman fortifications and various post-Byzantine churches, the most important of which is the 14th century **Church of Christou**, with some elegant and colourful frescoes. But also in the town, built in the square where tradition says that the apostle preached, is a grand outdoor marble and mosaic **monument**. One scene depicts him receiving his Macedonian call and another shows him preaching in Beroea.

For those who are interested in Macedonian history and discovery, **Vergina** will have a very strong attraction. It was just outside the small town, at the site of ancient **Aigai**, the first capital of the kingdom of Macedon, that during the 20th century some of the most momentous Greek finds were made, in particular the Royal Tombs of King Philip of Macedonia and other members of the royal family. Excavations began in 1976 and

Entrance to the Royal Tombs, Vergina

yielded unimaginable treasures. Among these were two gold caskets containing his and maybe even the queen's bones. In 1993 a **museum** was built on the site containing four separate tombs and a small temple built for Philip. Definitely not to be missed! Nearby are more tombs known as the **Macedonian Tombs**. A short distance from here, set on a mound, are the foundations of the **Palace of Palatitsia**. Though again there is nothing of any great height, there is enough to give an idea of the layout and enormous dimensions of the palace. A beautiful mosaic floor has been preserved. Although the palace is dated in the 3rd century BC, it is believed that the site may have been occupied as far back as 1000 BC. One can only guess at the wealth of treasures which may one day be unearthed.

Finally, the two other places previously mentioned as a possible part of a tour in Western Macedonia. The first is **Pella**, northwest from Thessalonika and once the capital of Macedonia. A royal city, it was the residence of King Philip and the birthplace of his son Alexander the Great in 356 BC, who was also tutored here by Aristotle.

The smallness of the site belies its ancient glories and should not, therefore, be underestimated. It is particularly famous for its pebble mosaics, some of the finest in Greece, both in the site itself and in the modern light, airy **museum**. Depicting mostly hunting scenes and dating back to about 300 BC, they are full of life and colour. Particularly outstanding are Dionysos riding on a panther, the Lion Hunt, and the Stag Hunt. Also to be seen are the **Agora** and the area where the shops were located. Excavations began in 1957 and are still ongoing, so there is much yet to be discovered.

It is worth driving on from here to **Edessa**, if only to see its **waterfalls**. The oldest remain to be seen is an arched **bridge** over which the Via Egnatia passed. But most people come here for the waterfalls which cascade down from the town to the valley below. In any case, after an early visit to Pella it makes a very pleasant coffee stop on the way to Veria and Vergina.

SOUTH TO ATHENS

If, like St Paul the Christian pilgrim has begun in the north of the country, then after exploring Thessalonika and Macedonia, it will be time to head south for Athens. One way to do this is by rail directly between the two cities, which is quick and convenient if there is pressure of time. However, if time is not a premium, then the alternative route by road is thoroughly recommended. Part of the attraction of this route is that it passes by Mount Olympus, a range of peaks spanning some 12 miles and the legendary home of Zeus and the other Greek gods. Another advantage is that you can stay overnight in Kalambaka and next morning visit the spectacular **Meteora Monasteries**.

So stunning is the first view of the rocks on which the monasteries are set that it is not easily forgotten. This amazing, sculptured formation of rocks rises up from the plain of Thessalia, with the monasteries perched among them like eagles-nests. Indeed, the very name 'Meteora' refers to the way in which they seem to be suspended in the air. Originally twenty-four in number, they date back to the early 14th century, but from at least the 10th century the rocks had been home to hermits. One can only marvel at the way in which they were built, with everything – stones, bricks, wood - hauled up by basket and rope ladder from the valley below. Today, however, there are only six which are accessible to the public, most of the others having fallen into disuse and ruin by the end of the 18th century. Please note that it is essential for visitors to dress appropriately, with no shorts for men and women, and no bare shoulders.

If you were to spend a whole day here it would be possible to inspect all six monasteries, but if on an itinerary you will have half a day at most to visit these gems, which have produced some of the finest pieces of religious art and craft. So, which ones should be chosen? Well, without doubt, the number one priority must be the

Meteora Monasteries

Mega Meteoron, the oldest and the highest, also known as the Monastery of the Transfiguration. Its domed church is truly glorious, with strikingly colourful frescoes depicting the history, dogma and liturgy of the Greek Orthodox Church. There is also a representation of Athanasius, the founder of the monastery, holding a model of the church. Other treasures on display are ancient manuscripts on parchment, silver liturgical vessels and very fine icons, dating from the 14th to the 16th century. As can be imagined, the views from Mega Meteoron across the area around are really quite something. By the way, if you wonder about all the steps up to the Monastery, well, just think that up until 1923 you would have had to go by rope ladders and then be hoisted up in a net!

Nearby is the **Monastery of Varlaam**, founded in 1518 by two brothers, but said to be named after the first hermit who lived on this rock in 1350. Situated in attractive gardens, the monastery's church is dedicated to All Saints and decorated with 16th century frescoes, which have subsequently been restored. Among the frescoes is one of the founders, Theophanis and Nektarios. Once again there are many treasures on view – crosses, vestments, sliver liturgical vessels, many scripts on parchment and hundreds of books. Also displayed in the museum is a Book of Gospels, dating back to the first half of the 10th century. On the outside of the building notice the ascent tower by which goods and people are still hauled up on a small cable car.

If visits to these two monasteries are not to be rushed so that their respective treasures may be savoured, there may not be time to visit any of the other four – **Holy Trinity, St Nicholas Anapausas, St Stephen** and **Roussanou/St Barbara**. But in exploring the first two at a leisurely pace, the Christian pilgrim will begin to appreciate why it is that the Meteora monasteries are so special. Interestingly enough, whilst not that many years ago there was only a handful of monks and nuns, and so it seemed, mainly for the benefit of the tourists, more recently increasing numbers have come to live, work and pray here, so continuing and enhancing the religious tradition of the monasteries.

It could be possible to do a long drive from here direct to Athens. On the other hand, it might be considered a wiser option again to break the journey by staying overnight in or near **Delphi**. The advantage of this is that you can visit the site first thing in the morning before the tourist coaches arrive from Athens, or even from the cruise ships that dock in Itea. An early morning visit is highly recommended, followed by the final part of the journey south into Athens.

Standing among hills and olive groves, the setting of Delphi is totally enchanting, to

Tholos of Delphi   © *alexstreinu stock.adobe.com*

such an extent that some would describe it as the most attractive Classical site anywhere in Greece. It is a claim difficult to refute. Regarded by the ancient Greeks as the centre of the world, Delphi was believed to be the home of Apollo, and individuals came from all over to seek guidance from the god about what courses of action they should take in particular circumstances.

To explore its beauty, start at the main entrance, which was once a market place, and follow the **Sacred Way** leading eventually to the remains of the Temple of Apollo. Originally this route was lined with something like 3000 statues and treasuries, so today's visitor must try to imagine how awe-inspiring the approach must have been. The treasuries were donated by various Greek city-states in appreciation for good fortune consequent upon favourable advice from the Oracle. On the left, on the way up, are the **Sikyonian** and **Siphnian Treasuries**. The route then takes a hairpin turn to the right and there on the left is the Athenian Treasury, the first Doric construction to consist entirely of marble. Though not a large building it is one of the landmarks of Delphi and was reconstructed in 1906. Adjacent to this is the **Bouleuterion**, the Council House, where policy was decided, and just beyond it the **Rock of Sybil**, where according to legend, the first oracles were chanted by the priestess.

Charioteer of Delphi   *Joyofmuseums*
                          CC BY-SA 4.0

Eventually, you arrive at the remains of the **Temple of Apollo**, built originally in the 6th century BC, but what is seen today emanates from the 4th century BC. From the Temple is a wonderful panoramic view both of the site itself and the region around. Reconstruction, particularly in the form of three huge Doric columns, gives some impression of the scale and grandeur of the building.

Further up the hill beyond the Temple is the magnificent **Theatre**, originally constructed in the 4th century but later remodelled by the Romans. Blending into the hillside it provides a most wonderful setting for the theatre, which held 5000 people. If you still have energy left, a climb up to the top tiers for further breathtaking views is encouraged.

But don't consume all your energy as you will need some for the walk up to the highest point of Delphi, the **Stadium**, the best preserved in the country. Every four years this was the scene of the Pythian Games, second only to those of Olympia. Poetry and music were also part of the occasion, for indeed, the games grew out of a music festival. Over 200 metres long, what is visible today comes from Roman times, with four remaining pillars from the Roman triumphal arch. As you look around you will notice that much of the seating is surprisingly well-preserved.

All the above relates to the upper part of the site, but if you retrace your steps to the main road and cross over, you will come to the lower part. Here is the **Gymnasium**, where athletes trained for the Pythian Games, and complete with the remains of changing rooms. But beyond this is probably the most beautiful of all Delphi's monuments, the circular ***Tholos***, once surrounded by 20 Doric columns but now with three re-constructed ones standing to illustrate its previous elegance. As well as the Sanctuary to Apollo, Delphi also had one to Athena. Set between the remains of two temples dedicated to the goddess, the *Tholos* dates back to the early 4th century BC.

Before leaving, a visit to the **Museum** is advised, for its contents are second in importance only to those of the Acropolis in Athens. There are sculptures, pottery, bronzes, friezes, all portraying the history and beauty of Delphi. But the highlight of the exhibition is undoubtedly the life-size Bronze Charioteer from the 5th century BC.

ATHENS

If this were a more general guidebook, Athens would warrant a whole publication to itself, there is so much to see and do. However, within the limitations of the purpose of this particular book, that it should be a portable and concise travelling companion for the Christian pilgrim, then it is only possible to highlight those aspects of the city most likely to appeal to a follower of St Paul through Greece and with limited time in Athens. For this new edition we have added a city plan, which we hope you find useful.

Though it has a history of more than 3000 years, the golden age of the city was during the great Classical period of ancient Greece. Having emerged as a growing power during the 6th century BC, it was the 5th century which witnessed the great flowering of art and literature and, of course, architecture, as under Pericles (495–429 BC) an ambitious programme of building was initiated. Yet during the era of Macedonian

The Parthenon

expansion, Athens became somewhat overshadowed and by the time of St Paul's arrival in the Roman age, it had lost most of its previous political power. It was, nevertheless, still regarded as the cultural and intellectual centre of the ancient world. But by the time of the Byzantine period, Athens was stripped of all its glory. So it remained until there was a revival of its fortunes in the 15th century after the Turkish invasion, and finally it began to re-establish itself on becoming the capital of Greece in 1834 after the War of Independence.

Although under the Romans Athens was no longer a political power with which to be reckoned, it still had its architecture and art as reminders of its glorious past. Temples, altars and statues still abounded, and it was this multiplicity of objects of devotion to which Paul referred when he addressed the Athenians from the Areopagus, alluding to an inscription he had seen on one of their altars, 'To an unknown god' (Acts 17:16–34), though no altar has ever been found bearing that particular dedication. The reference may mean no more than altars erected to nameless gods, and there is evidence that this was a practice in Athens at that time. Apparently Paul's preaching met with no resounding success, but it was not a total failure as he left behind some individual converts.

The **Areopagus** is the name of a small hill - 'Mars Hill' near the Acropolis - and in

The Areopagus

the Classical period is believed to have been the place where the Supreme Court met. In Roman times it was still the name of an assembly, but whose precise function is not clear. Possibly it exercised control over religion and morals, or had some jurisdiction over the various philosophers and teachers. Whatever the case, the only reminder of Paul's address is a bronze plaque on which the text from 'Acts' is inscribed.

From here is access to the **Acropolis**, a natural fortification with strengthened walls on which was built the 'upper city'. Now, as then, the Acropolis dominates the life of the city and wherever you are in Athens it seems you can never escape the looming presence of this great rock – your eyes always seem to be drawn towards it.

You enter the Acropolis proper through the remains of the **Propylaia**, the official grand entrance to the citadel. Regarded as a masterpiece of of Classical architecture, it was commissioned by Pericles and begun in 437 BC. To the right of the Propylaia is the **Temple of Athena Nike**, built between 427 – 424 BC, to celebrate victory over the Persians and dedicated to Athena Nike, the goddess of Victory. Destroyed by the Turks in the 17th century, it was restored two centuries later, with further major reconstruction in 1935.

Before moving on further, one other building should be observed from this entrance area. This part of the Acropolis affords the best view of the fine Roman **Theatre of Herodes Atticus**, built in AD 161 by the Roman consul, Herodes Atticus. Seating 5000 people it was originally enclosed under a cedar-wood roof. It was restored in 1955 and today hosts drama and music as part of the Athens Festival.

For most people the **Parthenon** symbolises not only the Acropolis but Athens itself. Built in 447 BC during the glorious period of Classical construction under Pericles, its ruins still stand today, though due to the ravages of weather and tourists it is no longer accessible to the public. Erected as a temple, it was dedicated to the goddess Athena the Virgin - *Athena Parthenos* - and contained a huge statue of her made from ivory and gold, of which a replica can be seen in the National Archaeological Museum. During the 5th century AD it became a Christian basilica and in Turkish times was used as a mosque, complete with minaret.

If the Parthenon is a 'must' so, too, is the **Erechtheion**, situated on the most sacred part of the Acropolis and believed to be where Athena produced the first olive tree out of a rock in her struggle with Poseidon for sovereignty of the city. Named after Erechtheus, one of the mythical kings of Athens, it is built on different levels and adorned with Ionic columns and beautifully decorated capitals. You will notice six draped female figures *(caryatids)* serving as architectural supports. These are exact replicas of the

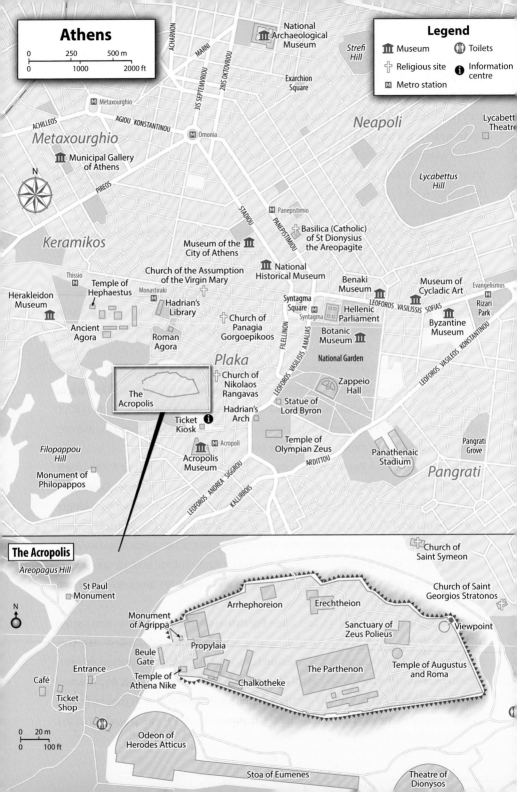

Athens

0	250	500 m
0	1000	2000 ft

Legend

- 🏛 Museum
- ✝ Religious site
- Ⓜ Metro station
- 🚻 Toilets
- ⓘ Information centre

ACHARNON
MARNI
3IS SEPTEMVRIOU
28IS OKTOVRIOU

Ⓜ Metoxourghio
ACHILLEOS
AGIOU KONSTANTINOU
Metaxourghio

National Archaeological Museum

Strefi Hill

Exarchion Square

Neapoli

Lycabett Theatre

Ⓜ Omonia

🏛 Municipal Gallery of Athens

PIREOS

N

Keramikos

STADIOU

PANEPISTIMIOU

Ⓜ Panepistimio

Lycabettus Hill

Basilica (Catholic) of St Dionysius the Areopagite

🏛 Museum of the City of Athens

Church of the Assumption of the Virgin Mary

🏛 National Historical Museum

Syntagma Square

Benaki Museum

Museum of Cycladic Art

Evangelismos

Rizari Park

Thissio
Monastiraki

🏛 Temple of Hephaestus

Ⓜ Hadrian's Library

Heidenreich Museum
Herakleidon Museum

Ancient Agora

Roman Agora

✝ Church of Panagia Gorgoepikoos

Plaka

FILELLINON

LEOFOROS VASILISSIS AMALIAS

Syntagma Ⓜ

Hellenic Parliament

Botanic Museum 🏛

National Garden

LEOFOROS VASILISSIS SOFIAS

Byzantine Museum

✝ Church of Nikolaos Rangavas

Zappeio Hall

LEOFOROS VASILEOS KONSTANTINOU

The Acropolis

Ticket Kiosk ⓘ

Hadrian's Arch

🏛 Acropolis Museum
Ⓜ Acropoli

Statue of Lord Byron

Temple of Olympian Zeus

ARDITTOU

Panathenaic Stadium

Pangrati Grove

Pangrati

Filopappou Hill

Monument of Philopappos

LEOFOROS ANDREA SIGGROU

KALLIRROIS

The Acropolis

Areopagus Hill

N

Church of Saint Symeon

St Paul Monument

Monument of Agrippa

Arrhephoreion

Erectheion

Church of Saint Georgios Stratonos

Sanctuary of Zeus Polieus

Viewpoint

Propylaia

Beule Gate

Entrance

Café

Ticket Shop

Temple of Athena Nike

Chalkotheke

The Parthenon

Temple of Augustus and Roma

0	20 m
0	100 ft

🚻

Odeon of Herodes Atticus

Stoa of Eumenes

Theatre of Dionysos

The Erechtheion

originals, which are now housed in the new Acropolis Museum, though they are only five in number as one was removed in the early 19th century by Lord Elgin. Somewhat smaller than the neighbouring Parthenon, the Erechtheion is no less majestic, having been extensively restored after it was all but destroyed in 1827 during the War of Independence.

Before leaving the Acropolis make sure you take in the views of the city around. But be warned – sometimes it can get quite breezy up here! To leave the site you have to take the same way back through the Propylaia.

While in the vicinity you might like to take a look at the **Theatre of Dionysos** on the southern side of the Acropolis and cut into the rock. The plays of Aeschylus, Sophocles, Euripides and Aristophanes were first performed here, so heralding the beginnings of Greek tragedy.

Not far from the Rock of the Acropolis, on the southeast side is the site of the **New Acropolis Museum**, opened in 2009. The previous one was on the Acropolis itself and begun in 1867 but over time became inadequate for the vast numbers of exhibits to be displayed. The new one has some ten times the capacity. On display are many original pieces from the Temples of the Acropolis, along with a re-creation of the original marble frieze in the Parthenon Gallery. Again, time will determine how much time, if any, you

The Theatre of Dionysos

can spend here.

Once you return to the city proper, make time to visit **Hadrian's Arch**. It marks the boundary between the old Greek city of Theseus and the new Roman city of Hadrian. Adjacent to it is the **Temple of Olympian Zeus**, the largest in Greece and larger even than the Parthenon. It was begun in the 6th century BC and completed by Hadrian in 132 AD. Only 15 of the original Corinthian columns remain, but their colossal height (58ft / 17.5m) helps to give some impression of the grandeur of the temple, which looks particularly striking when floodlit at night.

Museums are not to everyone's taste, but the **National Archaeological Museum** is probably one of the finest anywhere in the world. It has an excellent display of ancient statues, sculptures, Hellenistic bronzes and busts of Emperors. There is also a huge presentation of pottery, some of the finest pieces dating back to the 5th century BC. But the highlight of the Museum must surely be the Mycenaean collection, with quite stunning gold treasures dating from the 16th century BC, as well as the famous gold Mask of Agamemnon. The gold objects on display here are breathtaking and a tribute to ancient jewellers, potters and goldsmiths. The treasures on view are too numerous to detail, but in total present a wonderful exhibition of the history of Greek art.

Other **museums** which may interest you are: the **Museum of Cycladic Art**, a delightful display of the works of art produced in the islands of the Cyclades from about 3000 BC, with some exceptional small statues; the **Byzantine Museum**, covering 1500 years of Byzantine art with a splendid array of icons, ecclesiastical relics, and frescoes rescued from various churches; and the **Benaki Museum**, with a diverse collection of ceramics, carvings, costumes and jewellery, ranging from the 3rd century BC through to the 20th century, as well as some El Greco paintings.

Every visitor to Athens will want to discover the **Plaka**, one of the older parts of modern Athens. Busy, lively, bustling, it is not necessarily the tourist trap it is sometimes made out to be. Most people visit here more than once. The Plaka is rather like a large market, a good place to come and browse around the shops, some dealing in antiques and others in tourist souvenirs. You can also find many small studios where icons are painted using traditional methods. In addition to this, when you are feeling hungry there are plenty of tavernas where you can eat.

While in this region look for the tiny, domed 12th century **church of Panagia Gorgoepikoos**, next to the Cathedral and dwarfed by it. This really is a little gem and is sometimes known as 'The Little Cathedral'. In size it is no more than 7.5m x 12m (24.5ft x 39.5ft), which would probably have been appropriate in the 12th century when Athens was little more than a village. The outside is decorated with friezes and bas-reliefs spanning Classical to Byzantine periods.

Also in the Plaka is one of its favourite parish churches, **Agios Nikolaos Rangavas**, on the corner of Prytanaeiou and Epicharmou. Originally a Byzantine church dating back to the 11th century, rebuilt in the 18th and restored in 1970, it is a very popular place for Greek weddings.

If you have spare time in Athens and fancy a short cruise, **Piraeus** is, of course, its main port and one of the busiest in the Mediterranean. It is possible to take a day cruise from here to some of the nearby islands.

CORINTH AND THE PELOPONNESE

From Athens it is possible to make a day excursion to Corinth and either – or both – Epidaurus and Mycenae, via the **Corinth Canal**. Completed in 1893 after 12 years of building, it was the Emperor Nero who first had the idea of creating a canal to save ships sailing all the way round the Peloponnese. However, though the project was begun by him it was never finished. Unfortunately, it has never been wide enough to take the supertankers and giant container ships, although a few small – medium sized cruise ships have navigated with the aid of a tug. Smaller vessels can still be seen sailing through. It is possible to park nearby and look down some 90 metres on to the canal from the walkway across the bridge.

The major Christian site is, of course, **Corinth**, destroyed by the Romans in 146 BC, and then rebuilt as a colony a century later by Julius Caesar. It developed as a prosperous city due to its location between the Corinthian and Saronic gulfs, for bringing goods across the isthmus was the shortest and safest route between east and west. To save ships making the risky voyage around the Peloponnese, cargoes were unloaded on one side of the isthmus then carried over to the other and reloaded. At its height the city reached a population of 750,000 and excavations have demonstrated its extent, but it was eventually destroyed by earthquakes during the Byzantine era.

St Paul's founding of the church in Corinth is described in Acts 18. He spent 18 months here round about AD 50–51, practising his trade as a tent-maker to support his preaching mission, though once again he was not without opponents, both Jews and Gentiles. The population at that time was extremely cosmopolitan, consisting of Romans, Greeks and Jews, but the city had gained a reputation for its immorality. The apostle's first letter to the church here described a flourishing Christian community, in spite of the various problems referred to in his correspondences with them, for clearly

Towards the Temple of Apollo

70

Head of Dionysos mosaic

the 'first' letter available to us is not in fact the first that he wrote to them (see 1 Cor. 5:9). In addition to the various theological and moral issues raised in the letters, Paul also had to deal with challenges to his own authority as an apostle.

There are two parts of the site, ancient Corinth and Acrocorinth, the latter set on a hill some distance away from the main site. One of the most prominent buildings at the lower level is the **Temple of Apollo**, one of the oldest in Greece, dating from the 6th century BC and preserved by the Romans when they rebuilt the city in AD 44. There are still seven massive Doric columns standing. Another such structure is the **Temple of Octavia**, dedicated to the sister of the Emperor Augustus, but all that remains are three Corinthian columns.

It is also possible to make out the sprawling remains of the **Agora**, in which you can identify the location of some of the shops, as well as the Bema - or Roman Governor's tribune - before which Paul was brought when he was accused of sacrilege by the Jews. To reach the Agora you walk along **Lechaion Way**, which linked Corinth with the port of Lechaion. The road entered the city through a gateway and would have been bordered by shops. Just by the gateway is an attractive monument, the **Fountain of Peirene**.

Near the entrance and just south of the **Odeon**, is the **Archaeological Museum**,

Towards Acrocorinth

in which are displayed various discoveries from the site. There are statue heads, vases and 2nd century Roman mosaics from nearby villas.

All the time you are looking around Corinth you cannot but be aware of the towering presence of **Acrocorinth**. Whether you have time to visit once again depends on other elements of your itinerary if you are just on a day excursion from Athens. But if you are staying in the immediate area then more becomes possible. Entrance to the upper city is through three gateways – one Turkish, one Frankish and the third Byzantine. The whole place is surrounded by a formidable set of fortifications and within them are the remains of houses, churches and mosques. As you can imagine, the views all around from such a vantage point are stupendous.

From Corinth it is a short journey to **Mycenae**, and you may already have enjoyed its wonderful treasures on display in Athens. Represented here is a remarkable civilization spanning some 600 years from 1700–1100 BC. You will need to use your imagination to make the most of this forbidding citadel, for most of what remains is in the form of foundations. There is, however, the imposing **Lion Gate**, so called because of the sculptured lions above the lintel, and through which you pass into the stronghold. Here are **remains** of the Palace, royal graves, houses, and a flight of steps leading down to a

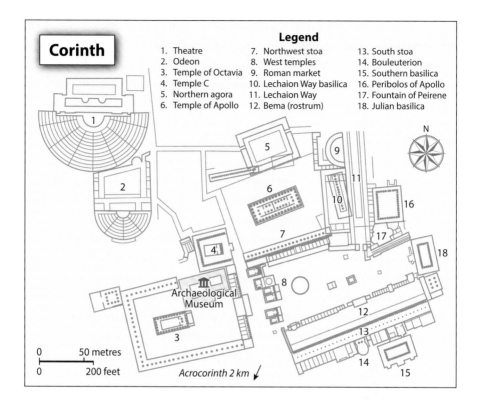

Legend

1. Theatre	7. Northwest stoa	13. South stoa
2. Odeon	8. West temples	14. Bouleuterion
3. Temple of Octavia	9. Roman market	15. Southern basilica
4. Temple C	10. Lechaion Way basilica	16. Peribolos of Apollo
5. Northern agora	11. Lechaion Way	17. Fountain of Peirene
6. Temple of Apollo	12. Bema (rostrum)	18. Julian basilica

Corinth

Archaeological Museum

0 ——— 50 metres
0 ——— 200 feet

Acrocorinth 2 km

cistern which was connected to a spring outside the citadel, so assuring those inside of a water supply during times of siege. Even if you don't visit the site make sure you visit the **Archaeological Museum**!

Whether or not Mycenae is on your itinerary, **Epidaurus** most certainly should be. A religious and therapeutic centre dedicated to the god Asklepion it is, however, probably most renowned for what could be described as the most beautiful of all **Greek theatres**. With 55 tiers of seats it is capable of holding 14 000 people. The lower 34 tiers are original and date back to the 4th century BC, while the upper 21 tiers belong to the Roman age. A unique feature is that of all the theatres it is the only one extant from antiquity with a circular orchestra. While you are here you may well experience someone demonstrating its incomparable acoustic, provided there is not too much hubbub from the other tourists! During a quiet spell, and there are not too many of those, you will be able to hear from the very top tier.

If it is possible to squeeze in a visit to **Nauplion** then do, even if just for a brief stop.

It is a thoroughly delightful and elegant little port overlooking a huge bay. Above the town and standing like a sentinel over it is a Venetian **castle**.

Hopefully, once you have explored this part of the peninsula, your drive back to Athens will be via the coastal route. It is extremely beautiful with wonderful glimpses of the coastline and leads you back across the Corinth canal.

PATMOS – The Island of St John

Having already referred to St John and his Letters to the Seven Churches in the chapter about Turkey, it is only appropriate that there should be some fuller consideration of this most delightful and important of islands. After all, much of the history of the island and its current appeal is bound up with St John.

Lying closer to the coast of Turkey than that of Greece, Patmos is an island steeped in religious devotion and with an enchanting landscape. According to Greek mythology, the island was a present from Zeus to his daughter Artemis. Findings of ceramics and stone tools indicate some habitation here in the Bronze Age (c.2000 BC). There is, however, little mention of Patmos by ancient writers and during the Middle Ages it seems to have been largely uninhabited till in 1088 the Byzantine Emperor, Alexios Komnenos, granted the island to a monk named **Christodoulos**. During the period 1207–1537 the island was subject to Venetian rule and from 1537–1912 it was occupied by the Turks. In 1943 the Germans took control but left in 1945, after which the island remained autonomous until 1948, when along with the rest of the Dodecanese it became part of the independent Greece.

A hilly, volcanic island, it is the northernmost of the Dodecanese islands, measuring little over 51 sq km (20 sq miles), and about 16km (10 miles) long (north to south) and 10km (6 miles) wide. Its natural beauty – with small beaches and coves as well as attractive villages - makes this a delightful island to visit, if only for a few hours. Yet its size belies its importance, as its strong links to St John make it a popular place for pilgrims. According to a **strong tradition** preserved by Irenaeus, Eusebius and Jerome, John was exiled here in AD 95. 'I John, your brother who share with you in Jesus the persecution and the kingdom and the patient endurance, was on the island called Patmos because of the word of God and the testimony of Jesus' (Rev. 1:9). The precise reason for his exile is unknown, but it may have been due to persecution as there is the possibility that the Romans used Patmos as a place of exile. We cannot be totally sure. Indeed, neither can we be totally sure who the John was, as Revelation gives few facts about the author's life, other than his Jewish background, and that he stayed here for

WHICH JOHN?

Since the 2nd century AD there has been a strong tradition identifying **John the Apostle** as the author of the gospel and letters of John, as well as Revelation, and many Christian pilgrims are happy to accept this tradition. Fair enough! There seems little doubt that the writer had great personal authority when addressing the churches in Asia and there are, indeed, echoes of the gospel. But as the style and content of Revelation are so completely different from that of John's gospel, and indeed, from anything else in the New Testament, it has been increasingly questioned as to whether the same author can be ascribed to both books. Some suggest **John the Elder** and others believe it to have been written by an unknown author to whom the name **John of Patmos** has been given. Maybe the most that can be said with any degree of certainty is that the author was a Jewish Christian whose name was John, writing towards the end of the first century, with some knowledge of the ideas in John's gospel and who was regarded by some churches in Asia Minor as a person in authority. What is more, he was writing against a background of Christian persecution during the time of the emperor Domition. He himself seems to have suffered for his faith and was writing from exile on the island of Patmos, though the degree of his personal suffering is not known.

about eighteen months.

Whatever the truth about the various candidates, there seems little doubt that Christodoulos turned the Cave where Revelation is believed to have been written into a place of worship and that he built the Monastery as a fortress in 1088. Archaeological findings indicate that it was built on the site of an ancient temple dedicated to the goddess Artemis, but later pulled down in the 4th century AD. So resolute was Christodoulos, that a greater part of the Monastery was completed in three years. In recognition of the religious and historical status of the Monastery, in 1999 the Cave and the Monastery were declared UNESCO World Heritage sites.

As well as its attractive landscape, the island exudes an atmosphere of religious history, some would even say tranquillity. As a cruise ship approaches Patmos, the sparkling white medieval town of **Chora** and its Monastery high above the town is

Monastery of St John, Patmos

the first thing that passengers see. Indeed, at first sight from out at sea the Monastery appears somewhat forbidding with its high walls and battlements, which was probably the original idea as a safeguard against attacks by pirates.

As there is no airport on the island, the only access is by sea and the deep-water harbour at **Skala** is where the ship docks. This is the main port and town of the island, which stretches round a wide, sheltered bay. This is a lively place with white houses, flowered courtyards, gift shops and boutiques as well as plenty of waterfront tavernas and cafés. It is interesting to note that around the 16th century it was one of the most important commercial ports in the Mediterranean.

If you are part of one of the organised cruises, then after you disembark, buses will take you up the hill towards **Chora** and near the entrance to the **Cave of the Apocalypse**. Be warned: the cave is accessed by 40 steps down and the same number up, but it is worth the effort to see the place and sense the atmosphere of the writing down of the vision. The entrance to the Cave is marked by a mosaic over the doorway depicting John dictating his vision to his disciple. Among other things visitors can see in the grotto is a rock which was supposedly a pillow used by John, and fenced off and outlined in beaten silver.

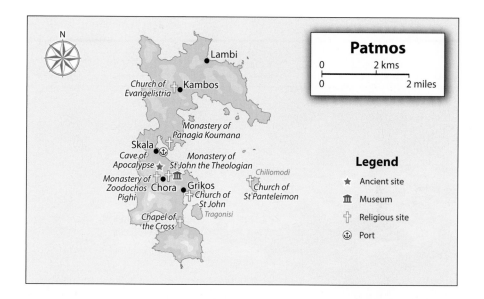

From here you walk up to the **Monastery of St John**, or as it is sometimes known, the Monastery of St John the Theologian, and it really is quite steep, walking over cobblestone paths. However, if you have to pause for breath from time to time it is a wonderful excuse to see some of the splendid views below you and out to sea. As you near the Monastery, there are about 90 strenuous steps to climb before you reach it, but well worth the exertion.

Though the Monastery from a distance has more the appearance of a fortress, once you pass through the heavily reinforced door on the north side, then you become aware of its religious character. The **main courtyard** is laid out in cobblestones and in the centre is a well with **holy water**. To the left is the **main chapel** which was erected in 1090 and as you face it there are four arched colonnades with wall paintings dated from the 17th and 19th centuries. Inside this main chapel is a splendid wooden **Iconostasis** from 1820, which replaced an earlier one from the 15th century. This, in turn, replaced an earlier marble one from the time of Christodoulos.

To the right of the main church is the **chapel of Christodoulos**, whose remains are said to have been buried here after his death. Also, there is the **chapel of the Virgin Mary**, with frescoes here and in the main church belonging to the 12th century. Hopefully time and interest will permit you to visit the **Treasury**, which houses a wonderful collection of icons, original manuscripts, silver and gold objects, sacred relics and

Skala, Patmos

vestments woven in gold thread, with embroidery decorated with precious stones. Also, look out for the 11th century parchment granting the island to Christodoulos.

Chora itself is the capital of the island, with narrow streets, whitewashed houses built in typical Aegean style, small white chapels, beautiful mansions, as well as restaurants, bars and small shops.

For those visiting the island from a cruise ship, time is limited depending on the particular sailing schedule. Whatever the time at your disposal, you are more than likely to return to the ship wishing you had much longer to savour the atmosphere of this most delightful of places.

OTHER ISLANDS

Readers of this book who follow the steps of St Paul and St John as part of a cruise will most certainly visit Patmos, but in addition may also visit some other islands. Which islands, however, depends very much on the particular itinerary of the cruise line at the time. This chapter, therefore, is designed to offer a brief introduction to some of the possibilities.

Knossos, Crete   ©*Iraklis Milas stock.adobe.com*

Crete

'I left you in Crete to set right matters which needed attention and gave you instructions to appoint elders in every city' (Titus 1:5). Titus had, of course, been a companion of Paul and yet in the narrative of Acts there is no mention by Luke of a landing on Crete. During Paul's final journey to Rome there is mention of his ship using the shelter of Crete in a storm and anchoring at the Cretan city of Fair Havens, but nothing is said about his spending time ashore. This clearly leaves the question hanging in the air, 'Did he or didn't he?' Certainly in Acts there is no reference whatsoever to Paul founding a Christian community on the island and if he had it would seem a very strange omission by Luke. There is, however, a tradition which suggests that Paul was released from his imprisonment in Rome and went travelling again, possibly to visit Titus in Crete. But we cannot be certain.

Be that as it may, Crete is the largest of Greece's islands and the fifth largest in the Mediterranean, with a total land area of about 8,300 sq km (3,200 sq miles). With its beaches, coastline and mountains, the island is a most attractive destination for tourists. Yet despite its development as a tourist island, Crete still maintains a great deal of evidence of its long and colourful history, with its Minoan palaces, Venetian towns,

Medieval castles, Byzantine monasteries and Ottoman mosques. From a cruise ship it is more than likely that the main site you will visit is **Knossos**, the largest Bronze Age archaeological site on the island. Minoan refers to the legendary king of Crete, Minos, and the Minoan culture is regarded as the earliest recorded civilization in Europe, from about 2700–1420 BC, with Knossos as its centre.

The Palace of Knossos was undoubtedly the ceremonial and political centre of the Minoan civilization and culture. An enormous site, it contained hundreds of rooms – store rooms, bathrooms, private apartments, public rooms and workshops, some containing huge pottery jars used to store olive oil. Also to be seen are the remains of a theatre and the Throne room. It is a colourful site with walls and pavements coated in a pale red colour and, of course, elegant wall frescoes. Nor must it be forgotten that Knossos was home to the Labyrinth, the dwelling of the mythical Minotaur. The Archaeological Museum in the nearby capital of **Heraklion** is one of the 'must-see' museums of Greece.

Rhodes

At approx. 77 x 37 km (48 x 23 miles) Rhodes is the largest of the Dodecanese islands and their regional capital. It is a fertile island with a rich variety of vegetation.

St Paul is said to have visited Rhodes very briefly in AD 51 (Acts 21:1). The local tradition is that he anchored at the small harbour of Lindos, in the southern part of the island, before sailing on to Patara and then changing boats at Phoenicia and heading for Tyre. Its location made it a major port on the ancient trade route through the Mediterranean and the Aegean and this continued for some centuries with both the Greeks and the Romans capitalising on its strategic location. The island was also famous for its Colossus, one of the 'Seven Wonders' of the Ancient World, a 32m (105 ft) brass statue of the pagan sun god 'Helios', which some say dominated the entrance to the harbour, while others believe it may have overlooked the port from the Acropolis of Rhodes. Constructed in about 292 BC the Colossus was destroyed by an earthquake in 226 BC.

The Knights of St John operated from the island from 1309-1522, before they later became sovereign over Malta (1530 – 1798). See also pp.85, 89. In 1522 the last Grand Master was compelled to hand over the island to Sultan Suleiman the Magnificent. Visitors these days cannot help but admire the medieval walled town with its palaces and 'inns'. The walls are in a magnificent state of preservation, with massive towers and bastions, as well as seven gates. Note the dry moat which was the first line of defence.

Palace of the Grand Master, Rhodes   © *filliposfilippou stock.adobe.com*

Among other things you will be shown is the wonderful **'Street of the Knights'**, along which several langues (orders) had their palaces with decorated portals and windows. At the end of the 'Street' is the stately and imposing **Palace of the Grand Master** which dominates the entire old town and which was the administrative centre of the Knights. Here are relics from the medieval period, as well as ancient sculptures and beautiful floor mosaics. A visit to the Old Town of Rhodes is a visit to be savoured.

Mykonos

Like Santorini, Mykonos has nothing to do with St Paul, yet they are islands sometimes included in the cruise ship itineraries. So a brief mention is made here just to fill in some of the background in case your particular cruise calls in at either or even both these islands.

Mykonos is an extremely popular tourist destination and is one of the Cyclades group of islands. It is, therefore, very cosmopolitan in character and with all its visitors the narrow streets can become quite crowded. **Mykonos Town** is its port and also its capital. A delightfully picturesque area, it has a maze of narrow streets, houses and churches, all based around its harbour in the middle of a wide bay. Here are boutiques, art galleries, bars, cafés and restaurants.

Mykonos

The area of **Little Venice**, first constructed in the mid-18th century, is particularly appealing with rows of fishing houses lining the waterfront, their balconies hanging out over the city. As you walk around, images of the famous Italian city are bound to come to mind, particularly the mansions with their colourful balconies and stylish windows. Keep an eye open, too, for the **church of Panagia Paraportiani**, a much photographed white church begun in the 15th century and completed in the 17th. In fact it is five churches in one and its white stones stand out against the blue sky.

Nor will you want to miss the island's famous **Windmills**. These are one of the most recognised landmarks of Mykonos, dating back to the 16th century. At one time they were a great producer of wheat and bread, but these days are a spectacle to be photographed. From here is a wonderful view down on to Little Venice, as well as being a good vantage point from which to view the sunset.

Santorini

This is the southernmost member of the Cyclades group of islands. Essentially, Santorini is what remains after an enormous volcanic eruption some 3,600 years ago at the height of the Minoan civilization. Once a single island, its earliest settlements were destroyed

Santorini

by the eruption and what is left is a huge lagoon surrounded by very steep cliffs on three sides. The centre of the island collapsed and so the sea rushed in to fill the void leaving what we now see – a crescent-shaped island.

Cruise ships anchor off-shore and passengers are transferred by local boatmen to the shore, from which you can go up to the capital **Fira** (*Thira*), by cable car, by donkey or even on foot. The town is perched on the stunning **cliffs** and from here are wonderful panoramic views of the coast. As can be imagined, in the summer its narrow streets are bustling with people. The architecture is very similar to that of the other Cyclades – low-lying houses, cubed in shape, made of local stone and whitewashed, and with the blue-domed churches it is a photographer's paradise. Tourism and agriculture are the mainstay of the local economy and it should not be surprising for the visitor to realise that it is also a very popular destination for weddings!

In 1967 excavations were begun at the site of **Akrotiri**, where they discovered an ancient Minoan city buried beneath the volcanic eruption of 1613 BC. The island's **Archaeological Museum** contains many finds from several excavations at Akrotiri, many of these finds dating from the 5th century BC to Roman times. Finally, in terms of the Christianisation of Santorini, this took place between the 2nd and 5th centuries.

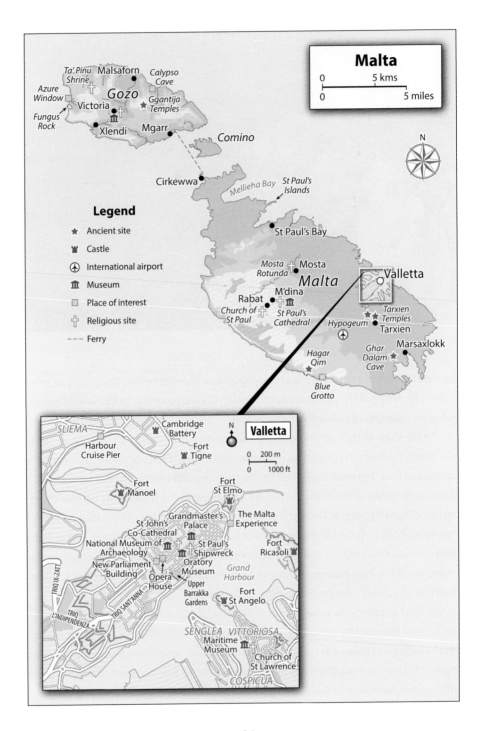

Malta

0	5 kms
0	5 miles

Ta' Pinu Shrine
Malsaforn
Calypso Cave
Azure Window
Gozo
Ggantija Temples
Victoria
Fungus Rock
Xlendi
Mgarr
Comino
Cirkewwa
Mellieha Bay
St Paul's Islands

N

St Paul's Bay

Legend

★ Ancient site
♗ Castle
✈ International airport
🏛 Museum
▢ Place of interest
✟ Religious site
--- Ferry

Mosta Rotunda
Mosta
Malta
Valletta
M'dina
Rabat
Church of St Paul
St Paul's Cathedral
Hypogeum
Tarxien Temples
Tarxien
Marsaxlokk
Hagar Qim
Ghar Dalam Cave
Blue Grotto

Valletta

0	200 m
0	1000 ft

N

SLIEMA
Cambridge Battery
Harbour Cruise Pier
Fort Tigne
Fort Manoel
Fort St Elmo
Grandmaster's Palace
St John's Co-Cathedral
The Malta Experience
National Museum of Archaeology
St Paul's Shipwreck
Fort Ricasoli
New Parliament Building
Opera House
Oratory Museum
Grand Harbour
TRIQ IX-ZAIT
Upper Barrakka Gardens
Fort St Angelo
TRIQ SANT'ANNA
TRIQ L'INDIPENDENZA
SENGLEA VITTORIOSA
Maritime Museum
Church of St Lawrence
COSPICUA

PART FOUR – ST PAUL IN MALTA

No more than 27km by 14.5km (17 miles by 9 miles) at its widest points, the island of Malta has a rich tapestry of history out of all proportion to its size. At a maritime crossroads in the Mediterranean, the occupying Phoenicians, Cathaginians, Romans, Arabs and British have all played their part in shaping its chequered history. Nor, of course, can the considerable influence of the Knights of St John be overlooked, who for nearly 270 years from 1530–1798, dominated the life and character of the island. For today's visitor there is still much to illustrate the influence of the Knights, particularly in Vittoriosa, their first base when they arrived in Malta.

That being said, much of the current character of the island dates back to an unexpected and accidental visit in AD 60, an event of no less significance for Malta than all its other momentous happenings. The preaching of St Paul in the Holy Land, and especially in Jerusalem and Caesarea, had caused so much opposition from the local religious leaders that he was arrested by the Romans, probably for his own safety as much as anything else. But at his trial Paul, as a Roman citizen, exercised his right to appeal to the Emperor, with the result that he and St Luke were shipped as prisoners from Caesarea to Rome.

However, during the journey the ship was hit by a violent storm just off the northeast coast of Malta and ran aground. Nevertheless, all 276 people aboard landed safely. 'After we had reached safety, we then learned that the island was called Malta. The natives showed us unusual kindness. Since it had begun to rain and was cold, they kindled a fire and welcomed all of us around it' (Acts 28:1–2). The rest of the chapter sketches an outline of Paul's three-month stay on the island and subsequent onward journey to Rome. Indeed, the whole story of the events leading up to Paul's arrest in Caesarea and eventual arrival in Rome may be read in Acts 21–28.

For the Christian pilgrim of today, the spot identified as the site of the landing is said to be **St Paul's Islands**, just off St Paul's Bay. There are two islands, the larger one of which has a very prominent statue of the apostle, commemorating the reputed spot where he stepped ashore. When the sea is not too rough it is possible to take a cruise round the islands from **St Paul's Bay**. Here, on the mainland of the Bay between Bugibba and Xemxija, is **St Paul's Shipwreck Church**, an elegant arcaded building reconstructed from the 17th century design, whose interior contains an inevitable painting of the shipwreck. It is said to be built on the site where the apostle was bitten by a viper, threw it into the fire and miraculously suffered no harm. A short distance away in the direction of Xemxija is Ghajn Razul, or '**the Apostle's Fountain**' where, according to tradition, St Paul either baptised the first Maltese Christian, or where he struck a rock and drank the water which came from it.

M'dina/Rabat

Not far inland is the 'silent city' of **M'dina**, so-called because for many years its narrow streets were regarded as unsuitable for traffic and even today only residents may drive in with cars. Once the capital of Malta, under the Knights it relinquished that status to Valletta.

M'dina is traditionally associated with Publius, the Roman Governor of the island at the time of Paul's visit, who welcomed the apostle to his home and offered him hospitality for three days. During this time the father of Publius was sick with a fever, but was healed by Paul. According to tradition, not only was Publius converted to Christianity but was also made the first Bishop of Malta.

M'dina

Legend has it that the present day Cathedral, **St Paul's Cathedral**, is built on the site of the house in which the father of Publius lived, replacing the first church built on the site in the 12th or 13th century and destroyed by an earthquake in 1693. Built between 1697 and 1702 by Lorenzo Gafà, the new Cathedral is regarded as his most outstanding piece of work and a superb example of Baroque art. Though the exterior has an impressive façade, fronted by a pair of cannon dating back to the time of the Knights, it is the interior which shows the building at its most splendid.

Designed in the shape of a Latin cross with a central vaulted nave and two aisles, the interior is richly decorated with paintings on the ceiling, the altar and in the apse, depicting various scenes from the life of St Paul, including the shipwreck. The colourful marble mosaic floor covers the tombs of some of the leading Maltese ecclesiastics and nobles. The marble font and the carved wooden sacristy both date back to the earlier Cathedral and are the only remains from it. Surmounted by a magnificent Baroque dome visible from and dominating the countryside for miles around, the whole building is an architectural and artistic masterpiece.

Also worth a visit is the adjacent **Cathedral Museum**, which contains much from the previous Cathedral, including Papal bulls and beautifully illuminated choirbooks dating

© nick stock.adobe.com

St Paul's Grotto

back to the 11th century. In addition, there is a splendid set of coins from Carthage to the modern, as well as woodcuts by Dürer and engravings by Goya.

Do allow time to wander round the narrow streets and soak up the atmosphere of this delightful place with its palaces, monasteries and churches. Make sure to find **Bastion Square**, because from here is a wonderful panorama of the island, encompassing both St Paul's Bay and Valletta.

Though larger in size and population than M'dina, the adjoining neighbourhood of **Rabat** (southwest) is in fact, a suburb. Tradition suggests that this was where Paul spent the three months of his stay in Malta and the deeply-rooted Christian beliefs of the Maltese people today clearly bear witness to the success of his mission on the island. In the heart of Rabat is **St Paul's Church**, reputedly built on the site of Publius's house and also said to be the first recognised parish church on the island. Below the church is **St Paul's Grotto**, where he is believed to have spent the winter of his stay. Here is a marble statue of the apostle and various frescoes.

A short distance away are the **Catacombs of St Paul** and of **St Agatha**, the latter having fled from Sicily to avoid her tormentors and taking up residence in Rabat. Both are full of tombs, niches and canopies cut from stone, which suggests that in the 4th and 5th centuries quite a large Christian community lived here though, of course, there is no direct association with St Paul himself.

Notice too, the dome of nearby (5km northeast) **Mosta Church**, a minor Basilica dedicated to the Assumption of St Mary and said to be the fourth largest unsupported dome in the world, and the third largest in Europe. Built in the 19th century its other claim to fame is that on the 9th April 1942, a German bomb crashed through the dome during a service attended by more than 300 worshippers. Remarkably the bomb did not explode and a replica of it, as well as photos of the damage caused, can be seen in the sacristy. Well worth visiting.

Valletta

With the arrival of the Knights in 1530, Valletta rather than M'dina was eventually to become the the the capital of Malta, but not until building began in 1566 on the orders of Grand Master Jean de Valette. Founded in the 11th century, the Order of the Knights of St John of Jerusalem was established principally to provide medical care for pilgrims to the Holy Land. But in time the role of the Order developed into a military task of fighting the 'infidel', with pilgrims needing physical protection as well as medical care. Eventually in 1291, along with the remaining Crusaders, the Knights were thrown out of the Holy Land, finally conquering and settling on the island of Rhodes in 1310. Here they stayed until 1522, when they were finally defeated by the Turks.

After agreeing an honourable surrender with the Turkish Sultan, Suleyman (known in the future as Suleyman the Magnificent), the Knights left Rhodes and were without any permanent home until Charles V, Emperor of Spain, offered them a refuge in Malta. So it was that in October 1530, under Grand Master L'Isle Adam, the Knights arrived at their new home and settled in Birgu (now Vittoriosa).

This area, known as the **Three Cities**, (Senglea, Cospicua and Vittoriosa) was regarded by the Knights as their capital and therefore the island's capital. So it remained until the Great Siege of 1565 when, under the leadership of La Valette, a totally outnumbered defence of Knights, Maltese militia, Spanish and Italian foot soldiers, faced an overwhelming number of Turkish invaders sent by Suleyman against an island stronghold which stood between the Turks and their domination of the entire Mediterranean Sea. Beginning in the May of that year, the siege was finally lifted in September after one of the most courageous defensive stands in military history. The Turks left, never to return and so, in the light of the siege, La Valette determined to build an impressive new capital which would also be a fortified stronghold. In May 1566 work began on building Valletta.

There are a number of remarkable churches in the city, but for the Christian visitor one most certainly to be visited is that of **St Paul's Shipwreck**, in St Paul Street. Dating back originally to the 17th century, the church is lavishly designed, especially the gold and silver of the ornate Chapel of the Blessed Sacrament. This was the work of Lorenzo Gafà, the architect of M'dina Cathedral, and his brother Melchiorre was responsible for the wooden gilded statue of St Paul, which is carried through the streets on the 10th February each year to commemorate the date of the shipwreck. The ceiling frescoes portray incidents from his time on the island. The Collegiate parish church also reputedly contains part of a wrist bone of the apostle, as well as a piece of the block from Rome

Grand Harbour at sunset

on which he is said to have been beheaded. Be that as it may, a visit to the church is not to be missed.

Another absolute must is **St John's Co-Cathedral**, because of the status and distinction it shares with the earlier St Paul's Cathedral, M'dina. St John's could be described as the Knights' own church, built by them between 1573 and 1577, and dedicated to St John the Baptist. It remained the Conventual Church of the Order until 1798 and was granted Co-Cathedral status in 1816.

On approaching the building, the exterior strikes the visitor as singularly unremarkable, but what a different impression once inside! Originally just as plain, the interior was designed in Baroque style by the 17th century Italian artist Mattia Preti, whose oil paintings depicting episodes from the life of John the Baptist adorn the splendid vaulted ceiling. The floor, too, is no less magnificent, paved with richly coloured marble tombstones of the Knights, each one decorated in mosaic with a knight's particular coat of arms. Also much in evidence is the eight-sided **Maltese Cross**, which was to become Malta's best-known face to the world. Side chapels dedicated to various saints commemorate the various langues (national groupings) of the Order. Everything leads the eye to the dominant raised high altar, made of marble, lapis lazuli and other semi-precious stones. It is indeed a masterpiece of a building.

If there is time, visit the **oratory** and **museum**. On display in the oratory is the now splendidly restored painting, The Beheading of St John the Baptist, by Caravaggio (1573–1610), probably the finest painting to be seen in Malta. The museum itself contains

an impressive collection of Flemish tapestries as well as vestments, illuminated choir scores and remnants of the church silverware not stolen by Napoleon in 1798.

Moving on from churches but staying with the Knights, a visit to the **Grandmaster's Palace** ought to be on the itinerary of every visitor. Though once the residence of the Grand Masters, most of it used to house the Maltese Parliament, with certain sections open to the public. Among the various exhibits on display, the most notable are the strikingly beautiful 18th century Gobelin tapestries in the Small Council Chamber upstairs; further along from here the Hall of St Michael and St George, with its frieze depicting the Great Siege; and the displays of armour lining both the upstairs corridors and also downstairs, taking pride of place in the Armoury itself (with one suit of armour worn by Grand Master Wignacourt weighing an incredible 50kg), along with an impressive collection of weapons from the 16th to 18th centuries.

A spectacular view of the Three Cities where the Knights originally made their base can be seen from the **Upper Barrakka Gardens**. There is also a Lift (elevator) here allowing access to the Grand Harbour. To the far left is the entrance to the Grand Harbour, and across the harbour and immediately ahead are the two peninsulas around which the Three Cities were established, with **Vittoriosa** and Fort St Angelo being very much the prominent features. Named Vittoriosa instead of Birgu to celebrate victory over the Turks, there is much here relating to the history of the Knights and a visit is recommended, but if there is time to visit only one of the cities, then without doubt this is the one to choose.

St John's Co-Cathedral

The **Church of St Lawrence** stands proud along the waterfront. Dating back originally to the 11th century, it was in due course to become the Conventual Church of the Knights before they transferred to Valletta. Much restored by them, its current interior appearance in the Baroque style again owes much to the work of Lorenzo Gafà in the latter part of the 17th century. The main altarpiece shows The Martyrdom of St Lawrence – another painting by Mattia Preti. The adjacent **Oratory chapel of St Joseph** contains a hat and sword of Jean de Valette himself.

While in Vittoriosa make a point of visiting the **Maritime Museum** which contains many maritime mementoes from Roman to British times, including models of the Knights' ships as well as the modern Maltese fishing vessel, the *luzzu*. Nor should the **Inquisitor's Palace** be missed. Whilst maybe not as vigorous as the dreaded Spanish Inquisition, nevertheless the aim was to guard against heresy and keep the Knights on their moral toes! Here men and women were imprisoned, tortured and executed. Restored since World War Two when it was severely damaged by German bombing, dungeons, cells and courtrooms are open to view, and some of the rooms in the Palace are lavish indeed.

But Vittoriosa should not be left without a closer inspection of its most prominent landmark, **Fort St Angelo**. It is possible that a temple was built on this spot in Phoenician times, followed by Greek and Roman ones, with the site eventually being developed as a fortress, particularly by the Knights when, during the Grand Siege, St Angelo became their command post. In similar fashion it was also to become Royal Navy headquarters in 1912, as well as surviving the German bombing in 1942. A walk along the wharf to the end of the promontory demonstrates the formidable scale of this imposing fortress standing guard over the Grand Harbour.

No visitor to Valletta should miss the opportunity of a cruise around the harbour, most of which begin from **Sliema**, a popular and fashionable resort, which at night-time provides wonderful views across Sliema Creek to the floodlit bastions of Valletta. Passing between Forts St Elmo and Ricasoli, the cruise enters the harbour and the imagination is fired by the stirring events of the past, especially when it was the base of the Mediterranean fleet in World War Two and destination for the Malta convoys battling their way through to maintain the survival of Malta, and so pave the way for an Allied victory.

Before leaving Valletta, those who have visited previously will notice the new **Gateway**, designed by Renzo Piano and completed in 2014, a project which divided the island and became a sore point due both to its modern design and the cost. As you enter you will see the new **Parliament building** on the right and the **opera house**, which is basically the restored ruins of the old opera house, making it an open-air theatre, though the stage can be protected.

SOUTHERN MALTA

The visitor to Malta would be unwise to neglect the southern part of the island for here, among other places to be visited, are some of Malta's remarkable prehistoric sites. Indeed, Malta's prehistory dates back to between 5000 and 4000 BC, when immigrants whose way of life was predominantly agricultural came from Sicily. It is these people who are believed to be the first inhabitants of the island.

The cave at **Ghar Dalam** (the 'Cave of Darkness') for example, dates back to these earliest times, about 4000 BC, and along with its museum provides a glimpse into the island's prehistory. It seems likely that at one time a land bridge existed between North Africa, Malta and Sicily, becoming the means by which various animals found their way across, particularly dwarf elephants, bears and hippopotami, the remains of which, along with those of humans, were found in the cave. Many of these animal remains can be seen in the adjacent **museum**. *[Temporarily closed for refurbishment at time of publication]*.

Not far away is the temple complex of **Hagar Qim** ('Standing Stones'). Somewhat younger than the Ghar Dalam site, Hagar Qim (about 3600 BC) is a marvel of prehistoric engineering. Built of soft limestone, the huge standing stones could more easily be decorated, but as a consequence have weathered badly. This impressive site, with its intricate design, prehistoric art and overall structure, bears testimony to a highly sophisticated society which originally planned and built it. If there is time, a short walk takes you to the **Mnajdra Temples**, set on a plateau overlooking the sea. Dating back to the same period as Hagar Qim, both these temple sites pre-date the Pyramids in Egypt by about 1000 years and appear to represent a community whose religion was based on fertility worship.

Both here and at **Tarxien** (just south from Valletta) will be found representations of the 'fat' goddess of fertility, sometimes unkindly referred to as the Venus of Malta. The **Tarxien temples** are younger than the previously mentioned ones (about 3000–2400 BC) and depict the peak of prehistoric temple building, demonstrated by the precise cut of the stone slabs as well as some of the finest examples of prehistoric art. It is worth noting that the altars, statues and friezes are all copies and that the originals are displayed in the **National Museum of Archaeology** in Valletta, which repays a visit to view these and other artefacts of Maltese history.

The nearby **Hypogeum** was a vast underground burial place built on three levels and dating back to around 3000 BC. Such is its importance that it has been declared a UNESCO world heritage site. Discovered accidentally by workmen in 1902, eventual excavations unearthed the remains of approximately 7000 people, along with pottery and jewellery. There is also an oracle chamber which suggests that rituals as well as burials took place here. Due to damage caused by the breathing of visitors, there is a strictly controlled micro-climate allowing a very limited number of visitors each day, and tickets need to be booked in advance (see also https://heritagemalta.org website). Nonetheless, as with Tarxien, some of the finds here are on display in the Archaeological Museum in Valletta – a further reason for a visit.

Whilst in the southern part of the island, do take in two other places. One is the **Blue Grotto** where, particularly in the morning light, those who take the boat trip into the caves will be rewarded not only by the beautiful blue of the Mediterranean, but the varying hues of colour reflected back from the water into the caves themselves. The other place is **Marsaxlokk**, Malta's largest fishing village where in the harbour the traditional Maltese fishing boats, the *luzzu*, bob up and down on the water. It makes an excellent lunch stop.

Before moving on to Gozo, two other visits are highly recommended. One is to **'The Malta Experience'** early on in any visit to the island. An audio-visual presentation, it depicts the colourful and stirring events which over the centuries have shaped Malta's past and present, so providing invaluable background information: https://themaltaexperience.com (see also https://church.mt | https://www.visitmalta.com).

The other is to one of the local **festas** which are held from May through till early October. These are colourful celebrations in many towns and villages, centred on the local band clubs. The churches are festooned with lights, flowers adorn the interior and the particular saint is paraded through the streets. The occasion is like an ongoing street party and firework displays are an integral part of the festivities.

GOZO

About one third the size of Malta, from which it is separated by a five-mile wide channel, Gozo has a distinctly different feel to it. Much less cosmopolitan than parts of Malta, it is very much a farming and fishing community. More sparsely populated than its sister island, Gozo therefore has a more spacious feel to it. Fewer people, fewer roads, fewer vehicles all contribute to an atmosphere of rural tranquillity, which the Gozitans are anxious to keep in spite of the number of visitors. A crossing of about 20 minutes by ferry from Cirkewwa in the north of Malta to Mgarr harbour on Gozo provides a most enjoyable day's excursion. What you see during your time on the island will depend on the particular itinerary selected by your tour company, or for individual travellers the time available, but the following paragraphs point to some of the main highlights.

The **Ggantija Temples** are believed to be the oldest free-standing monuments in the world and dating back to the period 3500-3000 BC, these temples are, therefore, of the utmost importance historically. As with the prehistoric temples on Malta, particularly those at Tarxien, the temples at Ggantija seem to have been places for the worship of a fertility goddess. Originally roofed-in, these two temples were constructed of limestone quarried from the hill opposite. The sheer effort involved in transferring the huge blocks of stone from the quarry to the temple site says much for their builders' engineering skills as well as their faith. As you wander around these temples you cannot help marvelling at the achievements of our prehistoric ancestors.

Ta' Pinu is a shrine of much pilgrimage, both now as well as in the past, a church within a church. The present building is in Romanesque style and dates from the 20th century and yet incorporates an original 16th century chapel named after a wealthy and devout man whose nickname was Pinu. Three centuries later, in 1883, a peasant woman walking past the church is said to have heard a voice commanding her to go inside and say three Hail Marys. From then on it gained a reputation for miracles, and so became a centre of pilgrimage where people prayed for miracles, and in 1920 building began on the present vast, cathedral-like church.

Victoria (Rabat)

Whatever else you see or don't see on a day excursion to this island, Victoria, the capital, is a certainty. You may still hear it called by its Arab name, Rabat (meaning 'the city'). The main focal point of attraction for the visitor is the Citadel, which, rather like M'dina's Cathedral, dominates the landscape around. So, too, just as from M'dina's ramparts there are magnificent views across Malta, from here also is a splendid vista over Gozo. The area of the Citadel is covered with narrow streets containing various places of interest like the **Armoury** and the **Folklore Museum**. But by far the main point of interest is the 17th century **Cathedral of the Assumption**, designed by the Maltese architect of M'dina Cathedral, Lorenzo Gafà. Though Baroque in style, this does not give the impression of being over-ostentatious as do some others. As well as the colourful floor decorated with the tombstones of bishops and priests, be sure to notice a remarkable trick of the eye. Though a dome was originally intended it was never finally completed. To remedy this defect a Sicilian painter named Antonio Manuele was commissioned in 1739 to paint an area of the flat ceiling to give the effect of its being a dome. Stand beneath it and look upwards and it has all the appearance of being a dome, so cleverly did the artist create the *trompe-l'œil* effect. There is also a **Cathedral Museum**, with a collection of vestments, silverware and paintings.

In addition to these main sites are a number of very pleasant ports of call, such as the fishing village of **Malsaforn** (Marsalforn) and the delightful bay of **Xlendi**, both making excellent lunch venues. Other possible stops are **Calypso's Cave**, where Ulysses is said to have had a dalliance with the nymph, Calypso, and the **Azure Window** and the **Fungus Rock**, the Window being a natural tunnel-like rock formation linking the open sea with a deep blue-coloured lagoon. The Rock is so-called because the Knights valued the fungus growing on it as a means of treating intestinal disorders!

The above description of Gozo assumes a day excursion from Malta, which is what the majority of visitors do. It is possible, however, to combine a stay on Malta with a few nights on Gozo.

The Blue Grotto © *Aliaksander stock.adobe.com*

Victoria (Rabat) © *Steven Santos stock.adobe.com*

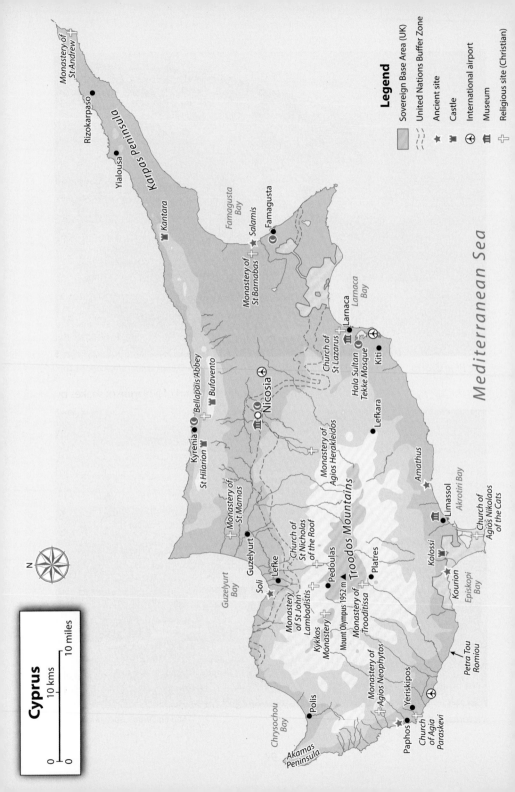

PART FIVE – ST PAUL IN CYPRUS

A BRIEF INTRODUCTION

The strategic position of Cyprus – just 65km (40 miles) south of Turkey and 105km (60 miles) west of the Syrian coastline – has always ensured its importance in world history. There are signs of settlements from the Stone Age, some going back as far as 7000 BC, and it is no surprise that the island plays a significant part in the development of Christianity.

The island had several Hellenistic-Roman cities by the time St Paul arrived, together with Barnabas and John Mark (he of St Mark's Gospel) in AD 45, having set out from Antioch and arriving in Salamis, where Barnabas had been born. They travelled on to Paphos, where Paul converted the Roman pro-consul, and before leaving to sail to Attalia in Turkey, they had established a thriving Church. Cyprus was also a natural stopping place for the early pilgrims to the Holy Land including the first of them all, St Helena, mother of Constantine, who had by then become the first of the Christian Emperors of Rome. She was there about 327 and famously rid the peninsula of Akrotiri of a plague of snakes by letting loose a thousand cats.

It was also a staging post for the Crusaders on their way to their major port of Acre, on the Mediterranean coast of what is now Israel. Berengaria, fiancée of Richard I (the Lionheart) of England, was shipwrecked with his sister, Joan, on her way to join him on the Third Crusade. The local ruler, Isaac Comnenus, was less than welcoming, so Richard had to take to arms to rescue his beloved, whom he then married in Limassol, on the 12th May 1191, and who thus became Queen of England. Whilst he was about it, he captured the rest of the island too, but sold it to the Knights Templar, who in turn sold it to Guy de Lusignan, a deposed King of Jerusalem, who had helped Richard defeat Comnenus and was a guest at the wedding, and who

Richard the Lionheart, on display in former St Peter & St Paul church, Famagusta

99

Lion of St Mark, Famagusta Citadel

was to have a more lasting effect on the development of the island. Although Guy died in 1194, the Lusignans established a 300 year dynasty. When the Crusaders lost Acre - their last remaining stronghold in the Holy Land – in 1291, they retreated to Cyprus, reduced the natives to serfdom and built the great castles of St Hilarion, Buffavento and Kantara on the mountaintops of the Kyrenia Range. They administered the island from the great castle at Kolossi, near Limassol.

The Kyrenia range of mountains is one of the three main physical features, as it runs almost the length of the Island in what is now North Cyprus. The Troodos Mountains to the south, dominated by Mt Olympus (1952 m/6400 ft), cover nearly half the total area of the Island, and in between is the fertile plain of Mesaoria.

The early Christian settlers, many of them refugees from the conquering Arabs in the Holy Land, were responsible for the building of hundreds of churches and monasteries, many of them beautifully adorned with mosaics and frescoes which are still a joy to see.

Cyprus bears all the marks of so many invasions, battles and civilizations. Phoenicians, Assyrians, Greeks, Egyptians, Persians and Romans have all left their stamp, and have provided the visitor with a wealth of history, architecture and art to marvel at. Turkish

Islamic rule over 300 years led up to British rule from 1878 until independence was granted in 1960. However, civic unrest leading to violence was not uncommon before and after.

Disruption continued with the fight over Enosis – union with Greece – culminating in a coup d'Etat that removed the President, Archbishop Makarios III – who had once favoured it. This precipitated the invasion by Turkey in 1974, as claimed protectors of the threatened Turkish Cypriot minority, the occupation of some 36% of the island and the creation of the Turkish Republic of North Cyprus. Some 150 000 Greek Cypriots were displaced from their homes in the north, while some 50 000 Turkish Cypriots went in the opposite direction. Democracy and Makarios were soon restored, however, to this day, Turkish troops are present in (if mostly confined to) a number of military barracks, as are United Nations peacekeepers along the buffer zone that runs parallel to the 'Green Line', and Greek units assisting the National Guard. The TRNC is recognised only by Turkey, with the Republic of Cyprus acceding to European Union membership in 2004 and EU law being immediately suspended in the 'occupied areas'. Sanctions on the import and export of goods make the north very dependent economically on Turkey – its currency is the Turkish Lira. Nicosia is the divided capital. Nevertheless, the divided island has remained largely peaceful and some scars at least seem to have healed over time. EU and UN funding has been used to restore monuments in both south and north, including at least some neglected, abandoned northern churches and monasteries, and southern mosques. There have been several attempts to reunify Cyprus, with a federation or two-state solution commonly proposed. Recent Cypriot presidents on both sides have been keen to progress matters, but their attempts in 2017 again failed. US Vice President Biden had visited both communities in 2014.

The north feels empty and underdeveloped, yet with a charm of its own, compared with the south, which has seen heavy development in some parts, with growing prosperity and increasing living standards following the adoption of the Euro as its currency. Like Greece, there was a Eurozone Crisis bailout but mostly confined to 2013. Meanwhile, the United Kingdom has retained its two Sovereign Base areas as a British Overseas Territory, which was part of the settlement of 1960. The total resident population including non Cypriots is probably over 1 million. Younger Cypriots on both sides born after the conflict try to make the best of their lives and do not appear to bear so many grudges, and so the future may lie with them alongside some real attempts at community cohesion. Who knows how quickly this text will become out of date, or whether the same situation stays for another 46 years.

CROSSING THE LINE – GETTING THERE

The opening of several more crossing points from 2003 has made travel much easier, including for the Christian pilgrim wanting to visit all of the sites mentioned in the Bible. Any such organised tour, however, will essentially be a two-centre holiday if your operator can be persuaded to deal with both Greek and Turkish Cypriot ground agents (buses and guides, not just hotels). The transfer from one to the other will probably involve driving up to a crossing point, disembarking, then walking across and (hopefully) being immediately met on the other side. For the independent traveller, if you want to use the same hire car, then you should start in the south, and pay the third party insurance (€20 at time of writing) at the crossing point – if you can cope with the idea of less cover than you might have on the same car in the south. You see many Republic-registered cars in the north, but not vice versa. Alternatively, separate rental in the north and south may be an option, subject to any drop-off fees, and working out airport transfer.

Passports are necessary but not visas. You may have to fill in a form at the North booth that they call a 'visa' which they stamp, and allows you a stay of up to three months. Always check before travelling to make sure no emergency restrictions have been imposed. There is effectively no duty-free allowance: just a packet of cigarettes and ¼ litre of spirits!

The main international **airports** are at Larnaca and Paphos. The north has Ercan Airport near Nicosia, which due to international sanctions can only accept flights from Turkey. Usually it is necessary to fly to Istanbul and either wait on the plane or change, the same for the return journey. Many Turkish Cypriots living in the north use Larnaca, which has a bus connection.

Apart from Nicosia (see pp. 114, 116) which is also best for reaching Kyrenia (Agios Dometios/Metehan by road), there are further **crossing points** at Strovilia for Famagusta, Pyla (closest from Larnaca and in the Dhekelia Base Area), Astromeritis/Zodhia from the Troodos to Guzelyurt, and Limnitis/Yesilirmak close to Soli and Kato Pyrgos in the northwest.

SOUTH CYPRUS
Paphos

Possibly the most attractive of the resorts, built around a picturesque **harbour** where pelicans wander among the café tables. Paphos is also important to the historian and the Christian visitor, for it was here that Paul and Barnabas had their significant clash with authority in the shape of the Roman pro-consul, Sergius Paulus, who was under the influence of a Jewish sorcerer called Elymas (or Bar-Jesus). The story is told in Acts 13 of how Elymas tried to turn the Consul away from the new Christian faith, but he was blinded by Paul, and the consul was converted. This was a significant step in the penetration of Christianity into the Roman Empire and also led to the dominance of the new faith in Cyprus itself, which by the 4th century had a great preponderance of places of worship.

Paphos was the centre of Roman authority, having been largely rebuilt after an earthquake of 15 BC. The Romans stayed until more earthquakes in the 4th century marked the decline of their power. In the meantime, however, they had built a large number of palatial **villas**, with some wonderful **mosaics**, many of which can still be seen. The extensive **Paphos Archaeological Site** (entrance close to the harbour) is within the area bounded by the **old City Walls**, which are partly excavated, and which contained the area known as Nea (or new) Paphos, running down to the port area. Four of these villas, in particular those of Dionysos, Theseus, Aion and Orpheus, should not be missed. Also at the site are other remains from the Roman era including the Odeon, a restored theatre from the 2nd Century, the **Asklepeion**, parts of the **Agora**, and the **Akropolis** – now topped by a lighthouse.

On the other side of the main Avenue Apostolos Pavlou which leads down to the harbour (officially part of the Archaeological Site but up the avenue from the entrance/car park, and take a right turn), are the sites of interest to the Christian visitor. In particular, **St Paul's Pillar**, which is, according to legend, where Paul was tied and received his 39 lashes. The adjoining **Church of the Blessed Virgin Mary** (Ayia Kyriaki Chrysopolitissa) is a 16th century building on the site of a much earlier basilica, the foundations of which can be seen. This was a very large building and there are some mosaics which date from the 4th century and some signs of a later Gothic church. The present church is shared by the English Anglican congregation and St Paul's Catholic Parish, each of which holds regular services at the invitation of the local Orthodox priest.

www.stpauls-catholic-parish-paphos.com | https://paphosanglicanchurch.org

St Paul's Pillar, church and basilica columns

Just further up the Avenue are the **catacombs and shrine to Agia Solomoni**. Solomoni was a Jewish woman from Judea, one of the earliest Christian converts on the island. It is said that her seven sons (the seven Maccabee brothers) were all martyred, buried here, and she was sealed inside alive. When the Romans returned years later, they found the young mother alive and drinking from a previously unknown spring, while a tree had grown bearing fruit. Votive rags hang above from the pistachio tree, which is believed to have curative properties for people with eye complaints. Down steep (and in places slippery) steps is a simple altar, fragments of 12th century frescoes, and with Crusader writings understood to be among the graffiti.

There are two castles in Paphos which should be seen. The **Byzantine Castle** which is passed en route to the Roman Villas, is partly excavated and restored, and dates from the 7th century AD. It once had 40 columns but was almost destroyed by the earthquake of 1222. Before that it had been surrendered to Richard the Lionheart in 1191. It is an open site but is not well maintained and care is needed when visiting it. The other Castle, or **medieval fort**, dominates the harbour and owes its present form to the Turks, who built it in 1592. Climbing to the top provides a splendid view, but there is little inside of interest today.

The main part of Paphos town is also known as Ktima, and lies uphill about a mile from the harbour. It has all the modern commercial facilities and also houses the major Museums. The **Archaeological Museum of Paphos District** (on Griva Diyeni) is worth keeping an eye on as it has a continually growing collection of archaeological finds, as digs continue in the area – in 2020/21 it was closed for re-construction and new presentation of its exhibits. The **Eliades Collection** – Ethnographic Museum – (Exo Vrysis) is a private collection lovingly put together in an old house, and includes some fossils which go back millions of years.

Between the old and new towns, a signed turning off leads to the **Tombs of the Kings**. An impressive group of burial chambers, some colonnaded, which date from the 3rd–2nd centuries BC. Although there were no kings of Cyprus at the time they were used, they must have been the final resting place of some very important people. Later they were also used as Christian burial grounds and as refuges from persecution. This is one of the locations where the pilgrim might envisage the difficulties that early Christians faced in establishing and practising their faith, difficulties that are present in parts of the world today.

Places near Paphos

On the coast road towards Limassol, the little village of **Yeriskipos**, two miles east, is worth a stop if only to purchase or sample the Turkish delight for which it is famous (though they don't call it Turkish any more). But it also has a small Byzantine church, that of **Agios Paraskevi**, which is probably one of the most interesting and attractive on the Island. It dates from the 11th century, has five domes, and some marvellous frescoes and icons. The frescoes depict various Biblical scenes and mainly date from the 15th century. There is a delightful little **Folk Museum** nearby.

Along this road, you can hardly fail to notice that the **legend of Aphrodite** is one upon which Cyprus depends for a lot of its folklore. Certainly all Cypriots will tell you that their Island is the true home of the goddess of love and beauty, from whom springs the very essence of the land. You will come first to the **Temple of Aphrodite** at **Palaepaphos** (now Kouklia), which was a very large place of worship, but a great deal has yet to be excavated. The site goes back to the 12th century BC. The temple was one of the most important places of pilgrimage in the ancient world, and was at one time a City Kingdom of itself. There is evidence of two Sanctuaries and some fragments of a mosaic floor. Further along the road, at **Petra Tou Romiou**, is the site known as Aphrodite's Birthplace, some rock formations on the beach where the Goddess is said to have emerged from the waves.

Enclistra, Monastery of Agios Neophytos

It is a very lovely spot, but even lovelier is the site of the **Baths of Aphrodite**, near Polis on the northern coast on the **Akamas Peninsula**. It will be about an hour's drive north from Paphos, well worth the effort. There are springs and pools set in woodland above the sea, shaded by a fig tree – the whole site is one of the most scenic in all of Cyprus and its romantic associations can only enhance the views. You can follow a walking trail for some 8km with stunning views of the coast, starting and ending at the legendary **Fontana Amorosa** (fountain of love). Alternatively, the site can be approached by a walk through a **botanic garden**.

Another worthwhile trip from Paphos is to the **Monastery of Agios Neophytos** 10km (6 miles) away and set on the mountainside where the Saint, upon arriving in 1159, dug caves in the rock to lead the life of a hermit. He was a preacher and writer, and some of his manuscripts survive in the monastery. You can visit the **Enclistra**, or Hermitage, which contains the tomb of the saint and is covered with magnificent frescoes, some depicting the saint himself, with the archangels Michael and Gabriel.

The Troodos Mountains, Monasteries and Churches

It is well worth hiring a car for a day or longer, to take a ride into the mountains both for the scenery, which is often stunning, but also to see some of the finest icons and frescoes of Cyprus in the ten churches which were designated by UNESCO as among

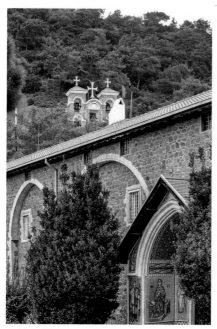

Kykkos Monastery

the finest World Heritage sites. The Troodos range reach their pinnacle at Mt Olympus. There can be winter skiing on the slopes and warm sunshine on the coast below - all on the same day at certain times of the year. There are many hiking opportunities on well marked trails, and crafts and delicacies to sample. But let us return to the heritage sites, several of which are grouped around the main resort, **Platres**, which is at 1200m (3900ft) and under an hour's drive from the coast. About 8km (5 miles) away is the **Trooditissa Monastery**, hidden in deep forests, and built in 1250 by two hermit monks after they saw a vision of the Virgin Mary and preserved an icon of the Virgin through several fires and other tribulations. The present building dates from the 19th century. There is an annual festival on 15th–16th August to celebrate the salvation of the icon. **Kykkos Monastery**, the largest of the group, is reached by a tortuous road, deep into the mountains, and again owes its origin to a hermit monk in 1100 who was presented with an icon of the Virgin Mary said to have been painted by St Luke. The icon miraculously survived several fires and is now covered in silver. It is said to have magical rain-bringing powers and so is much venerated by the local farmers. The **Museum** contains many more of the monastery treasures. Quite near here is the **tomb of Archbishop Makarios**, set among pine trees overlooking a grand panorama.

Visiting all **ten UNESCO churches** in the Troodos would take more than one day – especially alongside the other attractions of the region. Accommodation is available in or near most of the villages, though pre-booking and planning is advisable. Some churches are still within monastery complexes, but most nowadays are stand-alone. Many have pitched roofs with low-hanging eaves to guard against the winter snows. The frescoes collectively represent a mini course in church art, as they span several styles and centuries. If you are visiting Nicosia, be sure to include the Archbishop Makarios III Foundation Byzantine Museum (see page 114) where many of the churches' icons are displayed. During the long season, most are open – something that has not previously

St Nicholas of the Roof

been the case – but can close during lunch and at other times, so asking for a key at the nearest café might still be required. However, it should be noted that photography is strictly prohibited in many, though not all – pay attention to any signs by the entrances or ask. There are none of the list in Platres, however, if planning a complete tour that arrives there and goes on to Trooditissa, this is the order in which all can be viewed. Alternatively, the last churches on the list can be approached from Limassol and the sequence followed in reverse order.

Head for the attractive village of **Pedoulas** where the **Archangel Michael** (Archangelos Michail) is one of two churches – this in the lower part of the village opposite the **Byzantine Museum**. The artist, Adamos, painted in the post-Byzantine style, and so the brighter more evocative figures and scenes contrast with much of what will later be seen. We are in the Marathasa Valley and we arrive in the village of **Kalopanagiotis**, famous for its natural sulphur springs. Its **Agios Ioannis (St John) Lambadistis Monastery** on the other side of the river is, in fact, three churches under one large roof and offers at least two distinct styles of art in its Orthodox church and Latin chapel. The Italo-Byzantine style was popularised during the Lusignan and Venetian rule of the island. Head back towards Pedoulas, stopping at **Moutoullas** and the **Panagia tou Moutoulla** (Church of Our Lady) which was once a private chapel. Kykkos Monastery

Panagia Forviotissa

is off to the west of Pedoulas – an excursion in itself.

The most famous, and arguably the finest of the churches, is that of **St Nicholas of the Roof** (Agios Nicholaos tis Stegis) 2.5km (1 ½ miles) southwest of the resort of **Kakopetria** in the Solea Valley. It looks quite unlike other churches of the region, with its cream plastered stone walls and its roof of reddish brown wood shingles. Originally part of a monastery, it occupies a garden setting and the interior boasts some exceptionally fine frescoes, of varying date from the 11th to the 17th centuries. The style of painting appears less rigid than most of this genre and are the more attractive for it. Closed Mondays and public holidays. On the B9 road to Nicosia is found **Panagia tis Podythou**, just after the village of **Galata**. Founded in 1502 by a Greek officer in the service of James II, King of Cyprus, and originally part of a monastery, the Italo-Byzantine frescoes were added up to the 17th century.

Panagia Forviotissa – or **Asinou** – can be found by continuing north and then turning right off the B9. Close to the village of Nikitari in a beautiful setting, the church has a fresco depicting the Raising of Lazarus, among a near-complete covering of the walls, apse and ceiling – see whether you can see any part the artists have missed. The original artist painted in the style of Constantinople – which is where he is believed to have been from – during the 12th century. Then, back to Nikitari and continuing east and south for at least half an hour, **Timios Stavros tou Agiasmati** (Church of the Holy Cross) is in the Pitsylia region. Dating from the 15th century, this is another church whose walls, and here even the roof support beams, are covered in paintings.

The village of **Agros** makes a good base for the final (and also perhaps previous) leg of the churches tour. It is beyond the turning to the next church, **Panagia tou Araka** at **Lagoudhera** (25 minutes on from Agiasmati church) whose attractive roof forms a portico on three sides. The 12th century frescoes are of the late Comnenian style and so once again display the art of Constantinople, and one of the best collections of the middle Byzantine period. To **Pelendri** and its **Holy Cross church** (Timios Stavros), and we see a higher-looking well-proportioned structure without a sloping roof that supports three aisles. In fact this church has been much altered over the centuries. As ever, it is the interior that repays the visitor. While the frescoes are mostly 14th century – with examples of both the Constantinople and local Byzantine (Crusader and Armenian influenced) styles – fragments of the 12th century paintings can also be seen in the apse. Finally, on a quiet hill above **Palaichori** village, **Agia Sotira tou Souteros** (Transfiguration of the Saviour) feels like a discovery, as this small church has un-restored frescoes, iconostasis and carved door. The artist has mixed indigenous and Crusader styles, innocently drawing out of proportion figures with expressive features.

Limassol and Area

Limassol is a major resort with numerous hotels and a very long sea front - at least 8km (5 miles) of it. For all that, it is not so attractive as Paphos, if better located for exploration, and one has the feeling that the authorities could have done a great deal more to enhance the seafront with gardens and other facilities. It is the largest port - you can take short cruises to Israel or Egypt from here - and the second biggest city (after Nicosia). In effect, it became important after the evacuation of the Greek Cypriot population from Famagusta as part of the population exchange in 1974. It has an historic centre that will eventually be connected more easily with the modern marina. More noted for its night life, wineries and fine beaches (not to mention a zoo) than for its history, Limassol does nonetheless have quite a lot to offer the serious sightseer. **Amathus**, on the edge of the town, was an ancient settlement, and is partially excavated - where Berengaria was shipwrecked and blown ashore. The Knights of St John later made it their headquarters and it became a thriving city.

The present **Castle** dates from 1571 when it was rebuilt by the Turks, and it served as HQ for the British Army in World War Two. You can see the Great Hall and some cells from the time it was used as a prison. There is a very good view of the harbour from the roof. The **Medieval Museum** is a small but interesting collection within the castle, and there is also the **Limassol District Archaeological Museum** behind the main Public Gardens, which has a good collection of archaeological finds through pottery to jewellery.

Places to Visit near Limassol

A large part of the **Akrotiri Peninsula**, which almost adjoins Limassol, is British Sovereign Territory, being part of the military base ceded to Britain as part of the

Kolossi Castle   *Kourion*

Independence arrangements for Cyprus made in 1960. Much of it is thus out of bounds, but the **Lady's Mile beach** is excellent and almost deserted, and the **salt lake** is a magnet for bird watchers – it is peopled by migrating flamingos during the winter months. The **Church of Agios Nikolaos of the Cats** is a small monastic establishment which was founded in AD 325 after the visit from St Helena. Unsurprisingly perhaps, there are many cats to be seen here.

Back on the coast road towards Paphos is the imposing **Kolossi Castle**, the most important medieval castle in Cyprus. Isaac Comnenus, the local commander who was defeated by Richard the Lionheart, held court here and it then passed to the order of St John, whose authority operated through a feudal system of Commanderies, each covering a number of villages. Their huge estates included sugar cane production and vineyards, from which came the famous sweet red wine, Commandaria, which remains a favourite today. The **Lusignan Coat of Arms** is to be seen on the eastern side of the castle with four shields depicting the Kingdoms of Jerusalem, Cyprus and Armenia, plus the *fleur de lys* emblem of the Grand Commander, Luis de Magnac who oversaw the construction. The present edifice is just the **keep** from the 15th century, and it is entered by a stone bridge across the moat. The interior is rather stark, but the scale of the rooms is vast. Separately, the old **sugar refinery** is intact, and there are remains of the water mill and tower.

Further along the coast, at Episkopi, the next stop is at **Kourion**, a major attraction for all tourists. It is a vast site, and what you can see today is mostly of Roman origin, though its beginnings as a settlement were as far back as the 12th century BC. There are three main areas, the ancient city, the stadium and the Temple of Apollo (approached separately from the rest of the site). There is a **Christian basilica** dating from the 5th century, and a most impressive **theatre** overlooking the sea, which was only discovered and excavated in 1935. It now seats 3500 people for performances and concerts in a truly awe-inspiring setting. There is a great deal to see here, including a roman villa, baths, many mosaics, and the **stadium**, which has been partly rebuilt. The **Temple**, also partly re-constructed has a grand flight of steps and a colonnaded portico, but like much of this site, it was badly ravaged by earthquakes in the 4th century. When excavations began in earnest in 1876, they were financed by an American consul-general, and vast treasures of gold and silver jewellery were found, and immediately sent to the Metropolitan Museum in New York.

Larnaca and Area

The third largest city and a major resort, **Larnaca** also has the main airport of Cyprus. The two main reasons for visiting it are the **Church of St Lazarus** and the Pierides Museum. The Church is dedicated to the patron saint of Larnaca, as according to Orthodox tradition, he sailed into the port of ancient Kition following his resurrection by Jesus at Bethany. He met Paul and Barnabas who appointed him Bishop. He died and was buried again here, his tomb being discovered in AD 890. His remains were transferred to Constantinople, looted by Crusaders, transferred to France and then lost. The first church was built over the tomb, which is in the crypt, in the 9th century but has been rebuilt several times. The present one is a curious mixture of Romanesque, Gothic and Byzantine styles, with a 19th century bell tower. There are some remarkable icons, naturally depicting the Raising of Lazarus. The **Pierides Museum** started as a private collection in a private home, and contains a collection of archaeological treasures, from Neolithic times, including statuettes, pottery and Roman glass. It is one of the best museums in Cyprus.

Other sights include the **Fort**, the **Aqueduct**, and the **Archaeological Museum** with finds from **Ancient Kition** – much of which remains buried. The **Hala Sultan Tekke** (or Umm Haram) Mosque is one of the most significant sites for Muslims, as it contains the tomb of the aunt of the Prophet Mohammed. It is built on the site where she is said to have fallen from her mule and died. Constructed in the 18th century, the present mosque – recently restored in conjunction with St Andrews Monastery in the North – occupies a peaceful garden location by the **salt lake** near the airport.

Some 7 miles (11km) south of Larnaca, beyond the airport, is **Kiti**, a village known

Church of St Lazarus

mainly for its Church. Parts of **Panagia tis Angeloktistis** (church of the Virgin Mary, Built by the Angels) date back to the 5th century. Though it has been rebuilt several times, it is one of the oldest on the island, and its major treasure is a 6th century **mosaic** depicting the Virgin Mary holding the baby Jesus, with the Archangels Michael and Gabriel in attendance. The quality of this work still shows and it is claimed as one of the finest mosaics in the world.

Lefkara is a pretty village in the hills between Larnaca and Limassol. At around 500m (1600ft) it also supplies wonderful views of the mountains and distant coast, but its main claim to fame is for the making of lace. It is also known for its filigree silverware. You can see displays of both crafts at the **Handicraft Centre**, the **Museum of Traditional Embroidery and Silversmithing** and at various shops. The village houses are more reminiscent of Spain with their balconies, as are the narrow streets and courtyards. A most photogenic place. Leonardo da Vinci, on a visit to Cyprus in 1481 is said to have bought lace here for the altar in Milan Cathedral.

South Nicosia (Lefkosia)

The divided capital of Cyprus makes a worthwhile stopover, and visiting its museums complements your tours of the monasteries, churches and ancient sites. There are two **crossing points** to/from North Nicosia – both pedestrian only at time of writing – at the Ledra Palace Hotel and on Ledra Street. If you have a car for the duration and want to cross in Nicosia, then the Agios Dometios (or Kermia Crossing)/Metehan crossing is the only one to use – Metehan is less than 5km and 10 minutes' drive from Ledra Palace on the Turkish side.

The city has a pleasant **old town**, known as Laiki Yitonia, which has been well restored with a lot of arts and craft shops, cafés and galleries. The well-preserved **venetian walls** were completed in 1567, only three years before they were stormed by the Ottomans who took over the island. The famous **Famagusta Gate** is at the east side by Caraffa Bastion. The **Liberty Monument** on the Podocatoro Bastion is dedicated to the struggle against British rule, and independence. About half of the walls and their bastions are in North Nicosia.

The **Byzantine Museum – Archbishop Makarios III Foundation** (Plateia Archiepiskopou Kyprinou – within the Archbishopric) is a must-see with a priceless collection of icons. A further Byzantine museum is inside the **Archbishop's Palace**. Also here is the **Ethnographic (Folk Art) Museum**, which contains some excellent pottery, lace and embroidery. The **Cyprus Museum** (Loforos Mouseiou – Museum Street) is the national archaeological museum containing an extensive series of finds from the Neolithic to the Roman period. Figurines, statues – including a famous one of Aphrodite – pottery, gold and bronze objects are displayed over 14 rooms. There are several further museums, including the **Leventis Municipal Museum** (Ippokratous 17) and the **AG Leventis Gallery** (Leventis St. – ex. Leonidou St.).

St John's is the Orthodox Cathedral (reconstructed 17th century), was originally a Benedictine abbey founded by the Lusignans, and can be found in the Archbishopric. **Panagia Chrysaliniotissa** is understood to date back as far as the 5th century which would make it the oldest Byzantine church on the island. The iconostasis and several fine icons are the treasures of this interesting church. **Panagia Faneromeni** is the large church near Ledra Street crossing point. Rebuilt in 1872, the iconostasis is from the 17th century; the original icon of the Virgin is in the Byzantine Museum. The square also contains a school, library, and mausoleum for four priests executed by the Ottomans at the start of the 1821 uprising. The **Omeriye Mosque** (Platia Tillirias) is mostly used by the

Colonial style street, Nicosia   © *marinadastenko stock.adobe.com*

foreign Muslim population of the city, and was originally the 14th century Augustinian Church of St Mary.

St Paul's Anglican Cathedral is at 2 Grigori Afxenitou Street.

https://stpaulsnicosia.com

The Holy Cross Catholic Church is near Paphos Gate.

www.holy-cross-nicosia.com

South of Nicosia, in a garden setting near **Tamassos** – where there are some Royal Tombs – we find the **Monastery of Agios Herakleidos**. This church is dedicated to Herakleidos, who was chosen by Paul and Barnabas as their guide and companion. They appointed him Bishop, but after their departure from Cyprus, he was killed by pagans and buried here. His tomb is in the crypt and his skull is kept in a gold casket. The church was restored in the 18th century and is also a nunnery where the incumbents produce rose jams and marzipan.

NORTH CYPRUS
North Nicosia (Lefkoşa)

If you are in south Nicosia and wish to explore the north city, then the best crossing is Ledra Street rather than the one at Ledra Palace. The main **Market** (Belediye Pazarı) has an area selling souvenirs. The major interest for us lies in the former Saint Sophia Cathedral, which is now the **Selimiye Mosque**. It dates from 1298–1312 and the grandeur of the gothic interior, with its columns, is still redolent of the Christian cathedrals of this time. It has some grave stones from the Christian era. It became a mosque in 1576, and the Gothic west front is surmounted by two minarets. Another old church next to it is that of **St Nicholas of the English** (or **Bedesten**) which has a finely worked Gothic arch. The **Haydar Pasha Mosque** is formerly the church of St Catherine, and is the third impressive piece of Gothic architecture. At the rear is the former Archbishops House which is being used as a **Lapidiary Museum** with fine examples of stone work.

Just west in this restored part of the city, **Buyuk Han** is the largest Caravanserai on the island. A fine Ottoman building dating from 1572, besides providing accommodation it was used for trading. It was used by the British administration as a prison and restored in the 1990s. There is a galleried courtyard with fountain and a mosque – both originally for absolution. Now filled with stalls and shops, there is a row of old shops on the eastern side of the building. The **Buyuk Hammam** (Irfan Bey Sk 9) still functions as a Turkish bath, although it was built on the site of yet another former church, St George of the Latins – you can see at the entrance the old church portal.

The continuation of the **Venetian walls** with their bastions and gateways are a feature. Up near **Kyrenia Gate**, the **Mevlevi Shrine Museum** (Girne Cad) explores the spiritual traditions of the legendary Sufi whirling dervishes, from the mystical sect of Islam. During the summer there are regular performances of the dervishes back down near the Selimiye Mosque. On the way to the Gate or back, **Ataturk Square** contains the Venetian Column and former British colonial administration buildings.

Having covered both sides of Nicosia, we shall now deal with each of the remaining sites in North Cyprus in turn from south to north, east to west. It assumes crossing at Strovilia following a visit to Larnaca. Your first impression if coming this way well may be one of shock, even sadness, as it is here in the former renowned beach tourist hub of the island at **Varosha** – the southern quarter of Famagusta that once had a population approaching 40 000 – that you see the derelict high-rise hotels, barriers and fences, warning signs and a forbidding army barracks entrance. At least some of the beach,

Buyuk Han © *Conny stock.adobe.com*

along with hotels, elegant villas, main street complete with *'new'* cars in the showroom, and churches behind in the town, have all been off-limits since 1974.

Famagusta

A fortified town with immense walls and bastions, built by the Lusignans and strengthened by the Venetians. It became one of the major centres of Christianity after refugees arrived from the Holy Land from 1291 following the defeat of the Crusaders. They built no less than 365 churches, and substantial remnants of quite a number of them remain today. The major one, regarded as the finest Gothic church on the island, is the cathedral of St Nicholas, which is now better known – and used – as the **Lala Mustafa Pasha Mosque**. It was built in true Gothic style in the 4th century and the Lusignan kings of Cyprus came here to be crowned also as kings of Jerusalem. The triple-portal west front is surmounted by a minaret. The inside can be visited outside prayer times, and of course has no remaining Christian decoration, however, the soaring stonework and symmetry is there to be admired. The arched section of the former **Venetian Palace**, opposite the cathedral, interestingly has columns for added decoration brought here from Salamis. The attractive old centre offers several sipping and eating possibilities.

Lala Mustafa Mosque / former St Nicholas Cathedral

At the other end of these, **St Peter & St Paul church** was the Sinan Pasha Mosque, and with its flying buttresses and triple apse gives a strong impression of how imposing this entire city of churches must have been, especially when framed with the cathedral, and the surviving façades of other churches. This former church and mosque was being used as an exhibition space at time of visiting.

Parts of the old fortifications are now being put to good use as museums or arts centres, but the one of greatest interest is the **Citadel**, also known as Othello's Tower, which has a splendid 14th century Gothic Hall. Over the gateway is the Winged Lion of St Mark - the symbol Famagusta has taken to itself. Indeed there are several more to be seen inside the complex. It is generally thought that Shakespeare took the story of his Moorish king from the life of one Christoforo Moro, a Governor of Cyprus in the 16th century. There are excellent views of the coast, port and walled city.

Close to the west end of the fortifications, the **Nestorian Church** is intact and features rose windows, preserved belfry and triple apse. It is in the area of the city settled by the Assyrian Christians; after Ottoman rule it was used by the Greek Orthodox church, and now serves as a cultural centre. Close by you will find the single-aisled **St Annes**

Church with its classical Gothic west façade, yet here the bells have disappeared; it may have originally been part of a monastery.

Salamis and the Tomb of Barnabas

North of Famagusta straddling the coast, this is the major place of interest to those interested in history, and especially in tracing the early Church. The site of **Ancient Salamis** covers a large area, but with the most recognisable parts closest to the entrance. It was a Greco-Roman city, with some 100 000 inhabitants at its height, and most important of the city-kingdoms of Cyprus in the pre-Christian era. But its history goes back at least to the 11th century BC when it was populated by Achaean and Anatolian settlers. In Roman times it was known as Constantia, after being rebuilt by Constantine following an earthquake, and most of what remains today is of Roman construction. When Paul and Barnabas were here, it is reasonable to assume that they preached in the colonnaded **Forum**, and though much of the site has still to be excavated it is possible to visualise the streets, markets, and baths of the Roman city.

The most impressive remains are of the **Gymnasium** and **Palaestra** (wrestling school) with their own bath complex, and the **Theatre**, which has been partly reconstructed to house concerts and other events. There are marble columns and Roman statues (mostly headless), which make this a very impressive site and one of the highlights of a visit to northern Cyprus.

Further along the site, after the scant remains of a **Roman villa**, are the remains of two basilicas. **Agios Epiphanios** dates back to AD 400 just before the death of this Palestine-born Bishop of Constantia, and it was at the time the largest church in Cyprus. **Kampanopetra Basilica** is in a lovely position by the sea. The 4th century ruins are an impressive site of a large church with three apses, together with what is stated to have been a bath house (rather than a baptistery) behind – there are good remains of its mosaic floor.

Off to the right is **Silver Beach**, from where it is possible to swim on top of the submerged walls of the original harbour. By the time Paul, John Mark and Barnabas landed, a newer harbour had been built off to the left – both are inside today's lagoon.

We know that Paul and Barnabas moved on from Salamis to Paphos, and sailed from there to Perga, but we also know that Barnabas returned to Salamis at a later time, for he was martyred and buried under a carob tree at a site about a mile away. With him was buried a copy of St Matthews Gospel which he had always carried with him, and when his tomb was discovered and re-opened at the order of Bishop Anthemios

Salamis

following a dream, some 432 years later, it was found that the Gospel was intact. The Bishop obtained independence for the Church in Cyprus, granted in Constantinople by the Emperor Zeno, as the result of the discovery. The **Tomb of Barnabas** is now under a small **chapel** in an olive grove some 200 metres from the **Monastery of St Barnabas** – which is a more modern institution (from 1756) – and which contains a fresco of the Barnabas story and a collection of icons. There is also here a small **Archaeological Museum**, with a good collection of pottery and other items from the early Bronze Age up to 1200 BC. Three monks, all brothers, maintained the monastery from 1917 until their departure in 1976, however despite the occupation, the monastery was maintained and restored in 1991. The Saint's Feast day is June 11th and after a gap of some 30 years, the Mass and festival was resumed.

In the same area - for this was clearly a burial ground of the time – are the **Royal Tombs**. Around 20 burial chambers can be seen though at least 50 have been excavated and it is estimated that there are nearly 1000 altogether. They date from the Mycenaean era and a point of interest is that a number of apparent noblemen were buried with their horses, including harness, and chariots. One of the tombs (No 50) is that of **St Catherine**, a daughter of another Constantine, one of the Kings of Salamis, which is

St Barnabas' tomb

built like a church. She lived, was imprisoned and tortured for her faith – including being tied to a wheel – and died there in the early 4th century. Those of more humble birth were buried separately in the nearby **Cellarka Tombs** – rock-cut chambers – and their bodies scattered so that the tombs could be re-used.

As if that were not enough, also in the area 2km west of the monastery, the other side of the village of Tuzla is ancient **Enkomi** (Alasia) – the Bronze Age city which was linked to early Salamis and its later King Nicocreon (d. 320 BC) whose probable tomb is here. This was the mine and home of the wealthy metal – copper – merchants and whilst at the time it had its own inlet from the sea, Salamis was the main port. The spectacular artefacts of bronze, gold and ivory are in the Cyprus Museum in south Nicosia and the British Museum in London. This is an extensive site that will require at least two hours' exploration. And a village that can be visited as part of the tour of the area or on the way to the Karpas Peninsula or Kyrenia, **Iskele** (Trikomo) is 20 minutes north of Salamis. It has an **icon museum** in the church of Panagia Theotokos, plus a small **chapel** dedicated to St James that inspired Queen Marie of Romania (granddaughter of Queen Victoria) to build a replica in her gardens on the Black Sea coast.

The Karpas Peninsula

The **Monastery of St Andrew (Apostolos Andreas)** stands almost at the very end of the Karpas Peninsula (the *'pan-handle'* of Cyprus), and is a scenic two hour drive from Famagusta. With time permitting, however, there is much more to see on the way. On arrival, the site and the building will be seen to have benefited from extensive recent **restoration**. Greek Cypriot and Turkish Cypriot contractors were used, joint funding having been finally agreed between the Church of Cyprus, the Turkish Cypriot religious foundation EVKA, and USAID, under the auspices of the United Nations Development Programme (UNDP) – with Phase I complete. A beacon of hope for the future.

The story is that St Andrew was sailing back to Palestine when his ship was wrecked in the narrow channel here, partly because its captain had lost the sight of one eye. Andrew came ashore, thrust his stave into the rock, and out poured a stream of water, which proved to have healing powers, for the captain recovered his sight. A series of attested-to miracles followed, and pilgrims can partake of the water at a **fountain and chapel** near the shore (subject to Phase II of the restoration of the site). Most of the miracles involve curing complaints and diseases, and not only of the eyes. One near-contemporary miracle, however, concerns a woman called Maria Georgiou, from Cilicia in Anatolia, whose son was kidnapped in 1895. Seventeen years later, St Andrew appeared to her in a dream, telling her to pray for her son's return at the Monastery. So she set off on a crowded ship and told her story to another passenger, a young Dervish priest. When he asked whether her son had any distinguishing marks, and she described them, he tore off his clothes to reveal the same birthmarks, and thus mother and son were reunited. From that time onwards the site became a very popular place of pilgrimage for Greek Cypriots and Turkish Cypriots consider it a sacred place also. Since the crossing points were increased and restrictions eased, many Greek Cypriots have resumed making the journey, especially on August 15th – Feast of the Assumption – and November 30th – St Andrews Day. Here is also where it is understood Isaac Comnenus surrendered to Richard the Lionheart.

An earlier monastery stood on this site from the 12th century, however, the present church and buildings date from the 18th and 19th century respectively. The Church has some very old icons, all 58 having been restored in the project along with the belfry, and even the originally intended but not built north arcade constructed to complement the one at the west, together with a new chapel.

At the tip of the peninsula are some small rocky islands known as the Kleides (the

Karpas: Monastery of St Andrew © *erikzunec stock.adobe.com*

Keys). For those who have the time and the inclination, 5km away from the Monastery, **Golden Beach** is considered by some to be the island's best beach, with a long stretch of sand, few people and a small number of facilities. As with other relatively undisturbed beaches on the island, this is a nesting place for sea turtles. On the return journey from St Andrews (or on the way there), visits to **Agios Filon church** and the ancient city of Aphendrika – on the other (north) side of the peninsula via the central village of **Dipkarpaz** (Rizokarpaso) – are recommended. The church is ruined but much of the walls and domes still stand, while at the rear are the remains of a baptistery, and mosaics. Much of the site of ancient **Karpasia** and its Roman harbour are under sand and water. However, further on at the larger Hellenistic-Roman city of **Aphendrika** are the remains of another 10th century Byzantine church (Agios Georgios), together with the 6th century Panagia Chrysiotissa, and Basilica of Agios Asomatos; the city necropolis and citadel are nearby.

For really well-preserved mosaics and another – large – basilica flanked by the remains of its columns, head further down to Sipahi. **Agia Triada's** floors, along with geometric patterns and a message from the church's original donor, have images of a pomegranate tree next to a pair of sandals. Rather than one of the Biblical references to sandals, it is more likely a promise to the faithful of passing from this world to the next as the fruit was a symbol to Christians in the eastern Mediterranean of everlasting life. There are very small numbers of Greek Cypriots in some of the Karpas villages, who simply ignored orders to separate in 1974, with the same and other villages since settled by Turks from Anatolia. Sipahi is one of these. The villages of the Karpas do reward exploration for those with more time – the operative word, as the air is of a land where time has stood still.

Now, at the eastern end of the Kyrenia mountain range, we come to the easterly in a sequence of the three Crusader castles in northern Cyprus. **Kantara** stands at just under 700m (over 2000ft) and is some 68km (40 miles) to the east of Kyrenia. It was captured from the Byzantine ruler Comnenus by Richard I. It was abandoned during Venetian rule. Apart from some well preserved external and internal parts, one of the main attractions is the view, which can extend to Turkey and Syria if the conditions are right.

Kyrenia and Area

Kyrenia/Girne is the other main resort, on the northern coast, and is favoured on itineraries as the northern part of a two-centre stay, when combined with the south. It is set around a most attractive **harbour**, which is dominated by the **Castle**, a massive bastion, rebuilt by the Lusignans and further strengthened by the Venetians. The locals boast that in all its history their castle has never been taken by assault, though there have been several sieges.

On a steep climb of the castle, there is a Byzantine **church** dedicated to St George that was originally a basilica. Once inside the inner courtyard and parade ground, the main attraction is a museum dedicated to the **Kyrenia Ship**, the remains of a 4th century BC Greek vessel salvaged off the coast - one of the oldest vessels ever discovered and salvaged in this way. There is also a **display** of arms and armour, together with a number of archaeological finds. The view of the harbour and sea is wonderful. You will have earned your lunch or dinner.

The **old town** immediately behind the harbour has close to each other, **Agha Cafer Pasha mosque** dating from the 16th century and the **Chrysopolitissa church** which is probably older. There are many **Roman tombs** in the old town but most are closed off or have been built over. In front of the church overlooking the harbour, a house has been turned into an **ethnographic museum** and gives an insight into the trade carried on in the port, including the export of carob. The white painted Archangel Michael church is now the **icon museum** which displays icons rescued from various churches in the area over two floors, though many more were looted after 1974. **St Andrews** is one

Kyrenia Harbour

of two Anglican churches in North Cyprus (see also https://www.standrewskyrenia.org website). **St Elisabeth Catholic Church** (opp. the Dome Hotel) holds Mass in English– see Holy Cross Church, Nicosia. Apart from these places of interest and activities, the main attraction of Kyrenia is to while away time in the harbour or on the seafront, and take in this lovely location.

Of the Crusader castles, the most accessible is **St Hilarion**, which overlooks Kyrenia. Like the others, it was developed from the Byzantine fortress in the 12th century, over the grave of the Saint who had lived a hermit's life on the mountain until his death in the 8th century AD. It became a stronghold and an essential part of the Crusader defence of the island. They could send signals to each of these mountain top castles and from them survey virtually a whole swathe of the island. There are several associations in literature, film – if the association with Walt Disney as inspiring the castle of *Snow White* is true – and gaming. As the best preserved of the three castles, St Hilarion is built on three levels and it needs quite a lot of climbing to see it all, but the views to the coast are stunning. **Buffavento**, to the east of Kyrenia is the highest, set at 945m (3100ft) and is a little further inland looking out over the Mesaoria plain. Up here, you may discover why it is so named, as the strong buffeting winds come directly at you. To get to the remains

Bellapais Abbey

after parking involves a long climb up steps. It was used mainly as a prison, but like the other two castles, was largely destroyed by the Venetians in the 15th century who tried to defend the island at the coastal strongholds.

Bellapais with its Abbey will be a highlight of any visit, especially for those who have read and delighted in Laurence Durrell's *'Bitter Lemons'*. The Tree of Idleness which now stands within the garden of a restaurant of the same name cannot be the same one he described, but the atmosphere is there, even to the sense of indolence in the afternoon sun. The **Abbey** sits on its cliff top, some 400m (700 ft) above the sea and with a stunning view from its terrace. The Abbey dates from the 13th century when it was founded by the Augustinian order, and is built in Gothic style, with cloisters and a great vaulted refectory with a lovely rose window. The church itself has a number of very old icons and the whole setting responds to the name of Abbaye de la Paix – Abbey of Peace. It might just be a symbol for the bringing back together of the two communities that once lived here, and on the whole of Cyprus, in peace with each other.

But if you are interested to follow the stories of the saints, you may like to go on to the northwestern end of the island. With about three hours' driving time there and back, plus seeing the sights and having lunch, this is a full day excursion from Kyrenia.

Near **Lefke** are the ruins of **Soli**, which was a great Roman city of the 6th century BC. An amphitheatre and a Christian basilica are among the sites excavated. But also in that area, in the town of **Guzelyurt**, is the **Monastery of St Mamas**. He was a stubborn man, at least one legend states a 12th century hermit, who refused to pay his taxes, and the Byzantine Governor sent troops to bring him to Court in the capital. On the way they came across a lamb being set upon by a lion. Mamas sent the lion away, took the lamb in his arms, and carried it to the safety of the town – again, at least one legend states riding on the back of the tamed lion. The Governor was so impressed, that he forgave Mamas and released him from liability to pay taxes for the rest of his life. St Mamas thus became the patron saint of tax dodgers!

For full details of all the churches who hold services and Mass in English:

www.cypruscatholicchurch.org | www.cypgulf.org/cyprus

PART SIX – POSTSCRIPT
JERUSALEM TO ROME – JEW TO GENTILE

A book about "The Lands of St Paul", though on one level tracing the geographical travels of a very remarkable man, must also seek to represent something of the driving imperative behind them. Though it is beyond the scope of this volume to deal in any detail with the ultimate destination, Rome, yet given the extent of St Paul's ministry from Jerusalem to Rome, it is only fitting to conclude with some brief reference to his time in the capital of the Empire. After all, it was the Council of Jerusalem, described in Acts 15, which provided the impetus for the apostle and his companions to take the Christian message beyond the boundaries of Judaism.

The great dilemma facing the early church in that council was not merely to do with practicalities about the admission of Gentiles into the church, but with the very principle itself: should Gentiles be allowed to enter? That was the crux of the debate. Now if by some stretch of the imagination we can contemplate a negative answer to that question, then it is just conceivable that Christianity might have become little more than a localised sect within Palestine. However, once it was acknowledged that Gentiles as well as Jews had received the gift of the Holy Spirit, then the way was open for Paul to lead the advance from Jerusalem and take the Christian Gospel across barriers of race, religion, language and culture, so that far from being a localised phenomenon, it was to become a worldwide, all-embracing dynamic movement. From Jerusalem to Rome, from Jew to Gentile, such was its breadth.

After sailing from Malta, Paul and his companions put ashore in Italy at Puteoli, now Pozzuoli, the port near Naples then serving Rome. On their way into the capital by the Via Appia, they were greeted and offered hospitality by local believers. Acts 26: 13–31 deals with Paul's time in the city.

During his two years here, though under some kind of liberal house arrest, Paul had enough freedom to continue his preaching and teaching among both the Jewish and Gentile communities. How or when he was put to death in the city we do not know. Whether it was the culmination of his previous trials or some new accusation against him, we can only surmise. Maybe the details do not matter.

What is of paramount importance is the symbolism of Rome as the centre of the

Gentile world, to which Paul had given so much of his devotion and energy. By taking the Christian message from Jerusalem to Rome he became the catalyst by which the world vision of Pentecost in Acts 2 became a reality. So whether we follow his steps in Turkey, Greece, Malta or Cyprus, or even if we are fortunate, at some stage to all four, we are not merely travellers but pilgrims who hopefully will be infected by something of his faith, vision and commitment.

The colonnaded street at Ephesus

FURTHER READING

Here are a few select titles that have proved helpful to the authors:

Biblical
- Saint Paul: His Life and Work by Litsa I. Hadjifoti (Editions M. Toubis 2004)
- The Journeys of St Paul by James Harpur & Marcus Braybrooke (Putnam/Marshall 1997)
- Oxford Bible Atlas by Adrian Curtis (Oxford University Press 2007)

Archaeological
- The Glory that was Greece by J C Stobart (Sidgwick & Jackson, reprinted 1976)
- Greece: An Oxford Archaeological Guide by Christopher Mee & Antony Spawforth (Oxford University Press 2001)

Travel Accounts and Guides
- In the Steps of St Paul by H V Morton (Methuen London 2002 ed. and Da Capo Press Boston 2002 ed.)
- Catholic Shrines of Central and Eastern Europe by Kevin J. Wright (Liguori 1999)
- Greece: A Handbook for Christian Visitors by John D. Hayden (Honey Hill Publishing 2011)
- Christ in Glory: A Handbook for Christian Visitors to the Seven Churches of the Revelation of St John by John D. Hayden (Honey Hill Publishing 2011)
- Western Turkey (Cadogan Guides) by Dana Facaros & Michael Pauls (Cadogan Guides 1995)
- Malta and Gozo by Juliet Rix (Bradt Guides 2010)
- Bitter Lemons of Cyprus by Lawrence Durrell (Faber & Faber 1957)
- Cyprus by Josephine Quintero & Jessica Lee (Lonely Planet 2015)

Fiction
- The Kapillan of Malta by Nicholas Monsarrat (Cassell/Weidenfeld & Nicolson 1974/2012)
  Set against the background of the Second World War it is the story of a priest, Father Salvatore, who during the crucial period 1940–1942 holds his people together in the underground catacombs of Malta. Although a work of fiction, the story is interspersed with reflections on some of the great events of Maltese history, such as the arrival of St Paul and the Great Siege of 1565. A moving testimony to the island's suffering and courage, it provides a fascinating glimpse into wartime Malta.

INDEX